ADAM SMITH COLLEGE

T25127

10635291

WITHDRAWN

19/4/23

ADAM SMITH COLLEGE
LEARNER RESOURCES
SERVICE

The Chartered Institute of Personnel and Development is the leading publisher of books and reports for personnel and training professionals, students, and all those concerned with the effective management and development of people at work. For details of all our titles, please contact the Publishing Department:

tel. 020-8263 3387
fax 020-8263 3850
e-mail publish@cipd.co.uk
The catalogue of all CIPD titles can be viewed on the CIPD website:
www.cipd.co.uk/bookstore

LEADING HR

Delivering competitive advantage

Clive Morton
Andrew Newall
Jon Sparkes

Chartered Institute of Personnel and Development

© Clive Morton, Andrew Newall and Jon Sparkes 2001

First published 2001
Reprinted 2003

All rights reserved. No part of this publication may be reproduced, stored in an information storage and retrieval system, or transmitted in any form or by any means, electronic, mechanical, photocopying, recording or otherwise, without written permission of the Chartered Institute of Personnel and Development, CIPD House, Camp Road, London SW19 4UX.

Typeset by Fakenham Photosetting Limited, Fakenham
Printed in Great Britain by the Short Run Press, Exeter

British Library Cataloguing-in-Publication Data
A catalogue record for this book is available from the British Library

ISBN 0-85292-922-6

The views expressed in this book are the authors' own and may not necessarily reflect those of the CIPD.

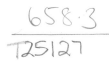

CIPD House, Camp Road, London SW19 4UX
Tel: 020-8971 9000   Fax: 020-8263 3333
E-mail: cpid@cipd.co.uk Webside: www.cipd.co.uk

CONTENTS

ABOUT THE AUTHORS

Dr Clive Morton is an independent adviser and coach on world-class strategy and board development and leads the Morton Partnership, which specialises in organisational transformation. He is a civil engineering graduate from Leeds University and spent the early part of his career in the British construction industry, working in both engineering and industrial relations. He also has a PhD in industrial relations from the London School of Economics. In the early 1980s he served as director of resources and administration at Wimpey Offshore and Wimpey Engineering, before joining Komatsu as director of personnel and administration at the outset of the company's UK manufacturing operations in 1986. In July 1992 Dr Morton was appointed director of personnel at Northern Electric. He was awarded the OBE in the same year for services to manufacturing and the community. He became personnel director of Rolls-Royce Industrial Power Group in April 1994 and then worked with Anglian Water from March 1996 until March 2000, first as human resources director and latterly as director of business development. Clive was a vice-president of the (now Chartered) Institute of Personnel and Development between 1997 and 1999, and is actively involved in a number of learning and innovation organisations. He is also chairman of Peterborough Hospitals NHS Trust. Clive is the author of two previous titles: *Becoming World Class*, which won the Management Consultancies Association prize for the Best Management Book of the Year, and *Beyond World Class*, both published by Macmillan. He may be contacted at info@themortonpartnership.com

Andrew Newall is the corporate human resources director for Allied Domecq, where he focuses on HR operations and the management of knowledge at the organisational level. His academic background includes a BA in social theory from Paisley College of Technology, an MA in employment law from Leicester University, an MBA from Warwick University and a diploma in personnel management from Glasgow College of Technology. He began his career in personnel with the British Steel Corporation at their Ravenscraig site, where he was employed as an industrial relations officer. He was promoted to the post of personnel manager for Whitehead Narrow Strip Ltd, a wholly owned subsidiary of British Steel. From there he moved to Llanwern Steelworks in south Wales before moving to Rotherham as project manager for the Narrow Strip business. In 1993 he joined Laura Ashley Ltd as human resources manager, initially responsible for their manufacturing units, before taking on responsibility for all activities in Wales. He was moved to Maidenhead as project manager to coordinate the HR activities arising from a global restructuring. In November 1995 he joined Allied Distillers Ltd as the employee relations development manager and was promoted to director in January 1998. He sits as a council member of the CBI and regularly speaks at management conferences.

Jon Sparkes is the human resources director of the Generics Group, an integrated technology and business consulting, development and investment company. His main focus is the growth and development of an organisation based on innovation and diversity. Jon graduated from Loughborough University with a BSc in management sciences, and gained his post-graduate diploma in personnel management at Nottingham Business School. He began his career in an employee relations role at GPT Business Systems (formerly GEC Plessey Telecommunications) during a time of significant change in the telecommunications industry. This was followed by several human resources roles within GPT, with a particular focus on manufacturing and IT. In 1993 Jon moved to Southern Derbyshire Training and Enterprise Council. His role included both human resources and operational responsibility for the TEC's interests in local economic development, labour market research and education. At this time he was a governor of a local further education college and one of the founder directors of Routes to Work (Derby) Limited, a company providing jobs and training for long-term unemployed people. Jon joined the Generics Group in 1995, initially as human resources manager, and in January 2001 he joined the group executive board shortly after its flotation on the London Stock Exchange. His role encompasses HR responsibility for all group operations in the UK, USA, Sweden and Switzerland. Jon is also a non-executive director of Opportunity Links, a not-for-profit business providing innovative social information systems.

FOREWORD

Success in the global, knowledge-based economy of the twenty-first century depends on people: how they are managed, how they are led and how they are enabled to contribute to business goals. World-class organisations excel in the delivery of customer value – which relies upon our profession's ability to deliver outstanding people management and development.

We are in a world where customers are firmly in control – in the public, private and voluntary sectors. Suppliers no longer dictate the customers' choice: customers demand satisfaction on their terms or they go to someone else. The expectations of customers are set by their experiences of the best. In such a marketplace, operational excellence no longer provides competitive advantage: it is an entry requirement.

This challenge to delight the customer can be all the harder for mature organisations. Established mindsets and sunk investment in equipment and working practices – combined with a lack of employee development and, worse, a resistance to sharing knowledge for fear of undermining management control – can leave a business powerless as the demands of customers are met by more nimble competitors.

Investment in unique technologies or products is not the answer either. The rapid, global spread of IT hardware and software enables many to match the physical products of the best. What sells is what comes from the brains and experience of the workforce, constantly adapted to new applications that the customer wants.

The answer lies in having the agility to meet the needs of the individual customer through rapid innovation and continuous improvement. This can be achieved only through the ability to capitalise on the knowledge, initiative and willing contribution of people at all levels of the organisation.

Two elements are critical here: first, the creation of a 'talent bank' of performing, motivated and continuously learning individuals;

second, leaders with the ability and the vision to create a 'can-do' culture and relationships of trust that will in turn drive the ambitions of the organisation ever higher.

World-class productivity and economic performance rely on the need to build human capital. To be an employer of choice means attracting and retaining people in tight labour market conditions and a commitment to develop them through continuous learning. The role of people management is to develop an innovative 'employer brand' that will attract talent and champion learning and development within the organisation. You have to invest in people: they are the primary sustainable source of competitive advantage.

Success depends, however, on volunteers, not conscripts. Every person in the organisation must make a *willing* contribution. 'Customer-driven' thinking has become central to the employment relationship – both employer and employee are now one another's customers. Developing and maintaining an effective psychological contract, valuing and respecting contribution from wherever it comes, is essential to support this new model of working.

Capacity through people has become the driver of strategy, rather than the outdated model that treats people as resources at the beck and call of the strategy of the day. An organisation can never know everything, so the notion of a top-down, rigid business strategy ceases to be applicable. Instead there must be fluidity in the strategy, both in where it originates and how it is managed. This can be achieved only with a team of skilled players with the ability to perform in a variety of positions, regardless of individual specialisms. The HR profession has to mesh with the strategic leadership of the business in order to realise the real benefits of the investment in human capital. But the new model doesn't just happen: it must be pioneered by leaders.

Leadership is central to the delivery of customer value, at both the strategic and operational levels. Leaders must aspire high and deliver results to *all* stakeholders by increasing customer satisfaction and growing revenues, not just by cutting costs. They must develop a culture that allows and encourages carefully developed human capital to work to its strengths. They must also realise that in such an environment of empowerment, strategy cannot be dictated from the boardroom but rather continually develops throughout the organisation as capacity through people rises.

Leaders also share the responsibilities of every other person in the organisation. They must keep close to actual and potential customers so that they know what delights them. They must track the competition, monitor developments in the market and ensure that this information is continually evaluated. They must foster learning at the workplace and the constant sharing of knowledge. They must establish conditions in which creativity is encouraged and rewarded.

Leading HR places the role of the profession today within this context. As the authors note, the notion of business partner has long been in the sights of HR professionals, but not enough have made it the reality. To become full business partners, we must demonstrate a clear understanding of the business, be prepared both to challenge and support the line, and to take a lead on cultural and change management issues. At the same time, we must continue to deliver efficient services, whether in-house or outsourced, and ensure that effective psychological contracts based on trust, respect and fairness are in place.

HR has always had an important role to play in business success. In this age of people-centred business strategy, the leadership offered by the profession has become critical. Organisations must have leaders who are able to build cultures that inspire people to contribute to the continuous improvement in the service given to customers. They must also have the capacity to manage the constant change that typifies today's business.

We as a profession are ideally placed to tackle these issues. It is for us to take up the leadership role and ensure that people can become the leading edge for any organisation. People will deliver this advantage, and thus the organisation will succeed, only if they are continually developed, supported, stimulated and given the freedom to perform against stretching goals. We as the people professionals must demonstrate that we are up to the job.

Geoff Armstrong
Director-General, CIPD

ACKNOWLEDGEMENTS

We would like to thank our editor, Robert Foss, for his great efforts in helping us produce a readable book in so short a time. The regular meetings and good follow-ups were essential ingredients in keeping the momentum going. We are also grateful to Geoff Armstrong for the foreword.

We all owe a great debt to our families and supporters for the indulgence of using precious 'home' time – we're not sure this is a good example of work–life balance! In particular:

Andrew – To Morag, Sean, Paul and David for having the patience to put up with me as I sat in the study for many a long hour. To mum and dad for the encouragement. To Ian Gourlay for his support during the years I had at ADL.

Jon – To Duncan Hine and Gordon Edge for supporting the contribution of ideas developed at the Generics Group, and to Annette, Sophie and Daisy for their personal support and tolerance, which made the writing possible.

Clive – To Florence for love and support, and to Lesley Sortwell for hard work and forbearance in helping shape the draft. To Amin Rajan and Mike Kinski for stimulation and comment.

INTRODUCTION

Can you identify with any of these put-downs?

> We have a 25-year apprenticeship around here – when you've been here that long we might listen to you!

> My secretary is late again today. Can you deal with her please?

> HR strategy is about paying 'X' off and taking 'Y' on – and keeping employee problems away from me! Change is what they have to do, not us!

> Can you deal with the people issues in the six minutes we have before lunch?

> I know we brought you in to change things, but we don't want to ruffle feathers, do we? There is an 'X' way of doing things.

If so, read on!

HR today, HR tomorrow

The HR profession has developed a unique tool-set based on its history in welfare, administration, industrial relations and strategic HRM. However, there is a sense among the authors that there is more to it than simply building a toolkit. The macro-economy has become global, and there is a clear movement to-wards networked organisations with complex structures, relationships and interactions with the environment. Organisations now more than ever need leadership in the organisational and people dimensions. Add to this the growing war for talent as organisa-tions seek to leverage competitive advantage by acquiring the very best people, and there is a clear role for the profession today and a leading role for it in the future.

The question will be whether the profession can rise to this chal-lenge. Having the toolkit is never enough; we need to ensure that we are at the table as true business partners – something we have been seeking for some time. In part, this is what this book is about. We aim to set out a proposition for achieving the position of true business partner – starting with the assumption that this will not simply be handed to the HR profession.

The background

All three authors have experience of the business partner position. Clive was one of the pioneers for taking HR to board level in the UK. He has seen the impact of strong and excellent HR input at the highest level in several large organisations. Andrew has taken initiatives in a wide range of areas, particularly in employer–employee partnerships and embedding learning into large and complex organisations. And Jon has led the HR aspects of a business during and following flotation in a sector where the war for talent is intense and global.

With Clive's facilitation, we set out to produce a book that is about leading from the front in our own HR functions and departments, and about leading our organisations as the people dimension becomes more and more important. Andrew and Jon have very different experiences, but as the book developed have discovered many common themes derived from this combined leadership role.

The book is definitely written from three different perspectives, and our intention was never to produce a textbook. However, we have tried to identify and draw out the common elements as much as possible. Ultimately our aim is to show how we have achieved business partner status for our HR functions in our respective organisations, as well as the context and circumstances leading to this.

The authors' perspectives

The authors have deliberately adopted different roles in the preparation of the book. Those roles are naturally based on experience, and we believe it leads to a balance that will suit the HR professional in the twenty-first century.

Clive has (by virtue of age!) the experience of seeing the HR function develop over the past three decades and has been heavily involved in the evolution of HR strategy related to business strategy. Sustainability is a key issue for business and HR.

Andrew brings a perspective that spans retail, manufacturing and heavy engineering together with the merging of differing cultures.

Jon brings a perspective of the new economy, with the significant involvement of science, innovation and entrepreneurial activity.

Andrew and Jon (through their experiences at ADL and the Generics Group – see below) deliberately provide a contrast, and Clive has been able to facilitate the golden thread whose purpose is to weave through the text to give a coherent message.

Allied Distillers Limited

Allied Distillers Limited (ADL) is the second largest Scotch whisky producer in the world and a subsidiary of Allied Domecq plc. It began operations in 1988 when the interests of George Ballantine & Son, William Teachers & Sons, Stewart & Son of Dundee and Hiram Walker & Sons (Scotland) were brought together. There was further expansion in 1990 with the acquisition of Long John International, bringing Beefeater Gin and Laphroaig Malt Whisky into the Allied Domecq portfolio. It produces over 10 million cases of Scotch, gin, vodka, liqueur and specialist products, over 90 per cent of them exported. ADL has 18 sites, many in remote locations, and employs approximately 1,000 people.

Change is no stranger to ADL. With merger and acquisition comes the inevitable rationalisation of activities. Much of the early 1990s focused on taking out excess capacity and streamlining both product and plant. The personnel function of the day excelled at this. What they did not tackle was the need for cultural change and the crying need to build emotional capital. The introduction of modern management practices and a focus on building commitment came later, but only after the human resources function itself was revolutionised.

The human resources team was at the heart of all the changes at ADL. The function played both a leadership role and a support role, depending on what was needed. Improved business performance has been the direct outcome of targeted training and development and the introduction of a leading-edge communication function. Much of the improvement was about catching up with the competition. This has been achieved. It's now about best-in-class performance. ADL remains on this path.

The Generics Group

The Generics Group was founded in 1986. The policy of the group is to invest in and commercialise underpinning technologies. This is achieved through the integration of advisory services, investment and the exploitation of new technology through licensing and the creation and development of spin-out companies.

Currently employing 300 people in Switzerland, the UK, USA and Sweden, the Generics Group floated on the London Stock Exchange in December 2000 at a valuation of £226 million. The company is growing rapidly through a combination of organic growth and acquisition.

With laboratories in Cambridge, Baltimore and Stockholm, Generics provides advisory and development services for international blue-chip companies, start-up ventures and other businesses. Services range from the development of products to provision of content-rich management consultancy services. The company employs high-calibre science, technology and engineering resources across a wide range of technical areas, and technology-qualified business consultants. Generics also generates a substantial amount of intellectual property, through a combination of employing creative people, providing an environment conducive to innovation, a strict policy of peer review and an effective means for rewarding commercial gain derived from innovation. The company has a unique innovative culture and free-market approach to project resourcing.

Generics also has expertise in the commercial exploitation of technology through licensing or spin-out creation and a strong track record of investing in third-party equity. The company spins out several companies each year, many of which remain majority-held subsidiaries for a number of years prior to Generics' exit. Employees are able to move from Generics into spin-out companies to take their innovations to commercial fruition. External resources are also recruited to quickly establish the spin-out companies.

The human resource strategies of the company encompass recruitment of very high-calibre people, the nurturing of an innovative culture, reward for innovation, career development in a non-hierarchical environment, the enhancement of international diversity and the sharing of commercial success with all employees.

Who should read this book?

Today technology and finance are no longer the limiting factors in building a unique and unparalleled business. Consider how much money was invested in the early dot.com rush. Investors were willing to throw money at them. What's more, how long did each survive? Today, good people are the limiting factor. If you have any interest in creating shareholder value, regardless of your professional discipline, you should read this book. This book is full of examples of the difference people can make and why the professionalism of the human resources function is a competitive weapon. Many organisations are waking up to the war for talent, the need to build emotional capital and the need to satisfy all stakeholders. The role of the human resources function is changing. Switched-on organisations recognise that people are at the heart of their success and as a consequence demand more from their HR function. HR professionals are now at the heart of decision-making. The CIPD has known this for some time and has recognised it by the inclusion of the HR executive at board level. If you have any interest in making your business a success or in pursuing a career in a discipline that will draw on all of your mental capacity, read this book and see what can be done.

Structure

❧ **Chapter 1** sets the perspective of HR today in its roots. We need to be cognisant of where the HR function has developed from, valuing its inheritance while coping for ourselves today in a very different world. The theory behind today's HR roles is explored, together with the dilemmas faced by contemporary HR professionals and line managers.

❧ **Chapter 2** deals with the challenge of sustainability, first in the context of rapid and radical change and its effect on organisations and those that work for them. The issues of competitiveness and survival loom large, and the chapter explores the experience of transformation in a number of organisations and sectors. Second, the role of the organisation within the economic and social context, and in particular the impact that HR can make to sustainability, is explored.

❧ **Chapter 3** describes the role of HR in today's organisation. Considering the nature of organisations, we argue that the role of HR must move ahead. Jon describes a role that takes the unique toolkit built by the profession and applies it to the needs of today's organisation. This includes the important paradox of providing support while challenging the business line management, and other key aspects of the role leading to the formal and informal position of business partner.

❧ **Chapter 4** explores culture. It is at the root of all things the human resources function is asked to address. It can be measured and changed. Cultural change, however, demands skill, and success can be guaranteed where that skill exists. The chapter includes practical steps in change management that, if followed, will help ensure success.

❧ **Chapter 5** shows that becoming 'best in class' requires organisations to relearn. This chapter draws on examples of how ADL went about relearning. Creating an attitude and hunger in people to learn new things is difficult but rewarding beyond the obvious. It is up to the human resources function to create an environment that both challenges individuals to raise their game and frees them from the fear of failure.

❧ **Chapter 6** looks at partnership, now a fashionable term. Many organisations fail to understand what it takes to build a partnership and the benefits that stem from a relationship based upon trust and mutual respect. Few know what it takes to sustain partnership. This chapter explains what actions ADL took to build and sustain partnership, and provides examples of steps others could adopt.

❧ **Chapter 7** tries to tackle the Holy Grail – the potential link between HR strategy and business strategy. First comes the recognition that strategy is not what it was, now that the world view is so disrupted. There is a recognition that there is no 'one size fits all' solution. We ask the questions: if the evidence of the HR contribution is so clear, why isn't everyone doing it? Why is HR strategy seen as rhetoric not reality? This chapter takes the opportunity to relate existing frameworks to Andrew's and Jon's experience as HR strategists in practice.

❧ **Chapter 8** looks specifically at the role of HR on the board. This is more than just the provision of a people input at board meetings. The chapter is based on an examination of the role of the board and its directors, with all of the inherent paradoxes, and in particular examines the role and responsibilities of the HR director, especially in matters such as board development and director remuneration.

❧ **Chapter 9** draws together many of the themes of the book while introducing the concept of employer of choice. The argument is put that all organisations should be striving to be employers of choice. All sectors have their own version of talent wars, and HR must lead from the war room. Employers have much to gain by meeting the needs of their people.

And finally...

This is a practitioner's book. It is founded on examples of making it happen in a wide range of businesses. It is optimistic and about 'can do', but essentially is about creating the right balance for HR and business, which are inextricably linked. It is not a 'best practice' manual. It is about sustaining and growing business through people in a practical way. We hope you, the people you work with, and your business all benefit.

Chapter 1

The changed role of HR in organisations

Clive Morton

I entered the personnel profession because it seemed a mess of interestingly intractable challenges. In the 1960s and 1970s, industry seemed in chaos due to people problems – or industrial relations, as we used to call them. Strikes were known as industrial action – a misnomer if ever there was one. It appalled me that the best of engineering, investment and intent was ruined by poor relationships, prejudice, elitism and adversarial attitudes.

Some of these evils are still around today, but expressed in different forms. Today's company suffers through lost talent, failure to generate ideas, lack of alignment and loss of opportunity and growth. The action may be individual, but the driver is still collective. Yesterday, both the action and the driver were collective, with trade union relationships at the fore. Today, the individual decides on levels of commitment and effort, although this is often dictated by collective cultures, which range from the risk-averse to the entrepreneurial.

The story of HR's roots in welfare has been well told, as has the branch line of administration. Yesterday HR was about managing a resource. Today it is about people being the only source of competitive advantage. It used to be simpler: business had an idea and the question was where to get the finance. Once the door opened we found the people. When business ran into trouble, the first casualty was training, followed by the trained workforce. Now it's complicated. In 1980, 20 per cent of company assets were 'intangibles'; by 2000, 70 per cent were seen by the City as intangibles – 70 per cent of company assets resided in the brains of employees, customers and suppliers.[1] Not only does (variable) productivity come from employees, but strategy and business development also come from intellectual capital – not the group-think of the corporate strategy function.

So what's the role of HR in this complicated new networked scene? Before we get to Jon's definitions in Chapter 3, we need to examine the different views of HR specialists and others. Broadly, there are three schools of thought.

From one perspective, the HR role is seen as a totem pole. This is a single-axis solution reflecting competition in the corporate hierarchy: how important is HR in relation to its peer functions? We can ask not only whether HR has a seat on the board, but also whether the CEO position is ever filled by an HR professional. We can also look at issues of relevance and connectedness – the links and dependencies between HR strategy and business strategy.

Another perspective focuses on the size and perceived influence of the function. Sometimes this measured clout will be affected by how much of the function is outsourced – in other words, what is HR left with? Some talk of the 'hollowing out' of the function: a residual head of HR deals with strategy with no real structure below him or her until the junior ranks are reached, while other tasks are absorbed by the line or outsourced. The traditional hierarchy is replaced by relationships in a matrix structure with other functions (usually line management), external suppliers or both. Relatively junior posts may still exist in HR, but there are real questions about how you develop careers and produce the HR directors of tomorrow.

Finally, an extreme scenario is gaining ground – operate with no HR function at all. This approach has existed for a long time. However, the rationale has changed. It used to be thought that people were not the real issue, so no specific help was needed beyond dealing with pay and rations. Now companies considering themselves world class have been heard to argue that HR is a line management function and that all managers should be people managers, since people are the most critical resource for sustainable competitiveness. This appeals to those who advocate ownership of the people issues and to enthusiastic cost-cutters alike.

But should the profession opt for functional redundancy? Is there not a conflict between the professional perspective, which seeks identity, standards, continuity and protection, and the hard-nosed commercial view of HR, which is all about added value rather than labels? The effects of some of the above solutions have been analysed in a recent study: *Tomorrow's Organisation: New mindsets, new skills* by Professor Amin Rajan and Kirsty Chapple at CREATE:

> Some HR people feel their craft has been undermined or demystified by the changes. Line managers are already overloaded and many are reluctant to take on HR functions. This has helped to create a gap between the values espoused by organisations' and employees' experiences.

This book is about how HR can best contribute to the success of business. The evidence is that there is not one set formula, but a variety of circumstances that demand separate solutions. We aim to help readers determine the appropriate solution for their own businesses and careers. But I want to start by providing a brief overview of my own career as a way of looking at the historical context.

When I began working, HR was seen as totally synonymous with one of the core issues facing the line – 1960s- and 1970s-style industrial relations. Yet all of this was transformed in the cauldron of the 1980s, when businesses in the UK were faced with two major disturbances. One was the impact of new competitive practices that affected the way they carried out their operations – the kind of lean production documented in *The Machine that Changed the World* by Womack, Roos and Jones (Rawson Associates 1995). Equally crucial was the revolution promoted by the Thatcher administration, which changed the role of trade unions in the UK. The combination of these two challenges shifted HR's priorities irrevocably from industrial relations to HRM.

A third factor in the coming of age of the HR function was the shift that put the people contribution, hitherto seen as a mere add-on, centre stage. The HR service has to be effectively supported, as otherwise it has zero credibility. Yet the tensions between managing the function today and steering the business of tomorrow represent the key dilemma for HR professionals and form one of the main themes of this book.

The evolution of HR – a personal perspective

A scenario from the 1960s

At the beginning of my career I was inspired by the credo of my professional body, the Institution of Civil Engineers, to 'harness the works of nature for the use and convenience of man'. My hero was the great Victorian civil engineer Isambard Kingdom Brunel, who achieved such fantastic things in such a versatile way. He wasn't a narrow specialist: he made things happen in both design and construction through other people – steering bills through parliament, finding the funding, overcoming opposition, thinking outside the box and so on. There was a downside, which came out later. Brunel died, burnt out, at the relatively tender age of 43; the safety record on many of his projects was hardly something we would be proud of today.

In my own more modest efforts to make things happen, I soon discovered there was both a human cost and a human limitation to physical progress. My first job as a graduate civil engineer was on Barbican Redevelopment in the City of London. The plan, which many found inspiring, was to restock the post-war bombed-out areas of the City with high-quality housing to complement and counter the ever-increasing demands for office space. It was to be an architectural icon, a development with its own theatre and concert hall, a stone's throw from the centre of the square mile. Technically it was brilliant. The architects Chamberlain, Powell and Bonn specified Penlee granite from Cornwall as aggregate for concrete so that when the surface was pick-hammered or bush-hammered, the whole structure would look as if it was hewn from the green granite. (After four decades of rainwater and London pollution, today's observers might be less impressed by the results!)

In the 1960s, unfortunately, the context was an overheated labour-intensive construction industry, where skilled labour was scarce and militancy was rife. Contractors had come to expect 'major problems' on large sites and indeed industrial relations in construction had reached the ultimate crisis point of government intervention. After just a few weeks on this exciting project it came home to me that however brilliant the technical and architectural concepts might be, they could be realised only through the effective organisation of the human input. Yet management was convinced that all the disruption was due to the presence of militants, agitators and subversives on site. All you had to do, it followed, was to prevent these undesirables from arriving and you removed the problem.

There *were* activists who saw the struggle on sites as part of a larger canvas – a class war. Others were just trying to protect and represent exploited labour. To observers it was bemusing. To me it was fascinating and compelling. I believed in achieving results via effective relationships, but there were none that appeared to work consistently in these situations.

Having studied industrial relations as a substantive part of my civil engineering degree, I was very curious to learn more. The phase of the Barbican project that I was on was run by John Laing Construction, which employed a labour relations officer (LRO) on site. Other contractors on other phases didn't have an equivalent. While they seemed to be in continual chaos, the Laing phase had far less disruption. My naive curiosity led me to ask about the difference – was it due just to the presence of the labour relations officer? – and to carry out an in-depth analysis for a PhD. I thus acquired a superb mentor in Professor Keith Thurley at the London School of Economics, who inspired a whole generation of personnel professionals. By examining some 4,000 different disputes on three major sites, I managed to put a whole new perspective on managing IR in construction. The headline conclusion was that, statistically, the number of disputes was in direct proportion to the labour members on site. Along with other evidence, this completely contradicted the received wisdom that issues were 'cooked up' by agitators and, in that sense, were not legitimate grievances.

At the time, I was in the happy position of being able to see both sides of the issue. As an engineer with no management responsibility, I realised that management's perceptions were myopic. As I wrote at the time about the Barbican:

> There were a phenomenal number of design changes. This created a disruptive influence on the progress of work in that not only were individual contractors completely out of control of the workload that was affecting them because of frequent design changes, but also craftsmen commonly saw their own handiwork torn down after it was completed, not because of poor workmanship, nor because of mistakes necessarily by the staff on the projects, but because of design changes that came through either after the work had been finished or too late to accommodate changes. This had a devastating effect on the pride that these workmen, and staff involved, had in what they were doing, and I am sure caused a great deal of militancy both on this site and on a neighbouring site that was used for comparative purposes.[2]

I felt that the method of employment and the myriad manipulated bonus schemes contributed to the lack of trust and dysfunction in IR when large numbers of people were employed on chaotic sites. In effect, management got the IR climate and the stewards they deserved.

There was no doubt that Laing's proactive practice of employing an LRO to record issues and to raise IR concerns as a crucial element in the management of the site meant that their handling of IR was streets ahead of comparable sites. Other contractors on site (Myton, Sunley) clearly underestimated the importance of industrial relations on the Barbican contract and the value of day-to-day control over labour relations. Sunley were prepared to 'buy' peace, as they admitted in their evidence to a court of inquiry. When the situation was clearly out of control they were prepared to go back on site agreements made only a week before and to undermine the authority of their resident contracts manager. Management were either totally unprepared or had clearly hoped that problems were something that were not going to happen to them.[3] Even Laing were not immune from disputes. It was in the nature of large industrial sites then; a policy of containment worked to an extent but did not solve the problem. I felt that the whole system was wrong: it was based on mistrust, labour was maltreated, poor organisation often exacerbated the issue, and there was no long-term commitment to training and security of employment. This vacuum was exploited by the activists for their own ends.

Fast-forward to the 1970s – in at the deep end

By the early 1970s I had decided to migrate from project management into full-time industrial relations (instead of just being an observer and researcher). I was approached to run IR for Tarmac in south London, where, as a result of an acquisition, I inherited two sites in Brixton, London Borough of Lambeth, that were already in difficulty from an IR point of view. One was dogged by continual disputes over two years, culminating in a five-month strike.

This time I was not observing – I was trying to stem the tide against, as it turned out, impossible odds. It became clear that the battles we were engaged in were little to do with the domestic issues of running the site. The prolonged dispute was aimed at our client – the moderate Labour administration at Lambeth – and was one of the factors that later led to the election of an extreme left-wing group in the town hall.

The changing context

This cameo seems a far cry from today's HR world and illustrates how much has changed – largely because set-piece collective bargaining has now been thrown into the dustbin. Nobody talked of partnership agreements in those days – the language was adversarial and, on both sides, the opposition was seen as subversive. This constrained both unions and management to act in ways that were not helpful to either of them.

The context has since changed enormously. In the 1960s, in accord with the 'voluntarist' view of industrial relations, labour issues were not planned for or understood. If a site was in trouble, it was the conciliator's problem. If it all went pear-shaped, the only recourse beyond the industry's conciliation machinery was that great British institution: a royal commission or court of inquiry.

In the 1970s things became more interventionist at industry level. In motor manufacturing, after three post-war decades of appeasement, the militants were challenged at last. In construction, the industry deliberately fragmented itself, with the growth of labour-only subcontracting partly aimed at defeating the militants (although this fragmentation has held the industry back commercially ever since). In the 1980s the Thatcher administration overturned decades of the voluntarist approach by tackling trade union power. The rest is history. Yet that still left the ever-present issue of motivation and productivity at employer level. How were we to establish effective relationships and deal with problems within a pluralistic framework?

Into change in the 1980s

It was significant that in the 1960s and 1970s the dominant management-speak was not about change. Industry was seen as part of a wider social order that was meant to operate mechanistically. The issues that concerned people were challenges to the social order, not the key issues that systems and attitudes were dysfunctional and that there was a long-term threat to competitiveness. Change often came via legislation, not from within.

I gravitated into the corporate sphere of people management, running IR and personnel for Wimpey plc, and I started to gain a perspective from the boardroom. I participated in the industry's national wage negotiations and disputes machinery. And I learned the value both of mentors and of lateral thinking in resolving issues that were often seen as intractable. As I recalled in *Beyond World Class*:

> My mentor was Ralph Cowan, a managing director of Wimpey. We were then building, with other contractors, the massive oil terminal at Sullom Voe in the Shetland Islands, and had quite sensibly agreed with the trade unions that, to minimise problems, with so many construction workers on a small island, wages, apart from 'beer money', would be paid directly into bank accounts. . .
>
> Problems arose when some construction workers queued for half an hour for their 'beer money' at the cashier's office. It was seen as a long time by them and their shop stewards and a claim was lodged for 'half

an hour's waiting time at cashier's office'. Following rebuttal of this claim, one of their number put in an individual application to the Procurator Fiscal in Scotland for payment of his wages, in full, in coin of the realm, as was his inalienable right, quite apart from any agreement between management and unions. To remove the issue from the Sullom Voe site, this individual was sent home to the mainland on full pay while discussions continued.

Readers familiar with the industrial relations scene in the 1970s will recognise the cameo immediately — how to get oneself in a corner with no way out. Capitulation was too horrible to contemplate: the transportation and containment of large amounts of cash on a small, remote Scottish island where relationships with the local population were already fragile; the contractors' reputation with the client, BP, one of the largest of the 'Seven Sisters' of oil production worldwide.

I can picture the scene now around the board table in Hammersmith, London, 500 miles from the hub of the problem. When I had apprised the board of the situation, Ralph Cowan, my mentor and boss, said to me, 'Has anybody gone to talk to the man?' (he was at home on full pay). We all sat in stunned silence at such naivety. Of course not; he had been put up to this by his peers and the shop stewards; no way would he make a decision on his own; in any event he was only a pawn — he had no sway or influence.

'Has anybody gone to talk to the man?' came the question again. All shifted uncomfortably in their chairs. Natural justice showed that Ralph had a point. Our mindset would not allow the question in. Ralph was the boss and had a razor-sharp mind. We had no better suggestion. With little confidence of a successful outcome, silver-tongued Arnold Nurick, my industrial relations manager for engineering, was dispatched to the Highlands. . .

Once the consequences of his actions were explained to our construction worker, he conceded it was not sensible to continue his actions with the Procurator Fiscal. He went back to work and peace reigned. I have never forgotten that example of Trinitarian thinking. I have also never forgotten that so many seemingly intractable questions can be resolved by face-to-face honest dealing with reality.[4]

Internal change is imported into British industry
In the mid-1980s, awareness of Japanese inward investment rolled out into the UK. It brought with it totally new perspectives —

upside-down thinking in so many ways. This was a turning point for manufacturing worldwide and for HR in particular. I was fortunate to participate in this revolutionary movement as the first employee of Komatsu UK in the north-east of England. I covered the experience in some detail in my book *Becoming World Class* (Macmillan 1994). The crucial difference as an HR practitioner was the role, scope and added value. Up to that point my role in companies was as part of a machined system to make it work, but not to rock the boat. No wonder I changed employers a few times: I believed the system was wrong and was determined to do something about it!

The Japanese surprised me. I expected, on visiting Tokyo in the early days, to find that I would be given a blueprint for HR in Komatsu UK. Not so. The then managing director of Komatsu Ltd, Tetsuya Katada, said that I must determine our policies with my colleagues in the UK – those that would be right for that factory, its employees and for competitiveness. The only thing they would insist on from Tokyo was an adherence to the Deming principles of total quality. Wow!

Some of the results of this experience are developed in Chapter 2 of this book. For the purposes of this chapter, the significance was the major change in my role as an HR practitioner – I was catapulted into HR policy and strategy inseparable from business strategy. From the perspective of the twenty-first century this is now de rigueur. In 1986 it was a brave new world.

Missionary work in the 1990s

After six exciting years helping to create a real solution to perennial problems in UK manufacture, seeing people develop and the company achieve long-term profitability, I was tempted to try some of the solutions in a UK 'brownfield' industry. First at Northern Electric, newly privatised, then at the Rolls-Royce Industrial Power Group and latterly Anglian Water. I also provided input as a non-executive director in the NHS (for further detail, see Chapter 2).

In parallel with changes in the economic and social context, I found my own role changing dramatically. The IR experience of the 1960s and 1970s was in the context of institutions. The 1980s experience with Komatsu was about bottom-up change. In the 1990s it was clear that established companies could not just cherry-pick good practice and expect permanent results. Importing 'total quality' on its own without changing culture and behaviours was worthless. My focus then went to the boardroom. It was clear that change had to be led and had to happen at the top for any long-term benefit. It was also clear that the balance between HR and their peer group had to change. People problems could no longer be seen as 'HR's responsibility'. Other managers and directors had to take a 'people view'. This led to questioning – what, then, is the specific role of HR? And what did we require from the echelons of middle management, which had been continuously downsized in the 1980s, described as 'blockers' or 'corporate concrete'?

At last in the late 1990s academic studies started to converge with practice. The socio-technical theory and human relations school of the 1960s and 1970s was seen by many practitioners as too soft and fluffy and unfocused on results. It took Deming and Juran, with their rigorously statistical approaches to quality control, to introduce managers to issues of trust and 'driving out of fear'. Well-founded research in the UK and USA showed that HR practices led to increased productivity and profit.[5]

Until recently, however, there has been little academic contribution on the developing role of HR. Dave Ulrich, professor at the University of Michigan, broke new ground in *Human Resource Champions* (Harvard Business School Press 1997) with his helpful quadrant for analysis (see Figure 1).

This framework mirrors my own experience. In the 1960s and early 1970s I was locked into the bottom right-hand quadrant dealing with IR issues. In the late 1970s and early 1980s my interest spread into the bottom left-hand quadrant and some of the top right-hand. Komatsu in the late 1980s gave me the opportunity to complete the quadrants with its heavy emphasis on the top left-hand quadrant of strategy via change. Yet although this model is useful for HR professionals, Ulrich also

Figure 1

HR ROLES IN BUILDING A COMPETITIVE ORGANISATION

Reprinted by permission of Harvard Business School Press. From *Human Resource Champions* by Dave Ulrich. Boston, MA 1997, p24. Copyright © 1997 by the Harvard Business School Publishing Corporation; all rights reserved.

stresses the importance of 'HR with attitude' – success is about energy and intervention as much as about work classification and it depends crucially on the perceived credibility of HR. This theme is developed further by Andrew and Jon in their contributions to this book.

What does the HR role look like in the twenty-first century?

To most involved in today's HR, its role appears confusing. In the 1970s and 1980s HR was a fringe activity in business – often, as described in the IR scene earlier, in the cauldron of events and crucial to problem-solving, but rarely in the centre of policy or strategy. Small wonder it became known as reactive. Then business discovered how central people were to competitiveness. Suddenly this was an area to invest in – training was an investment, not a cost. HR departments grew in size and importance. The logic of engaging the peer group of managers and directors in people issues emerged, and with the increasing pressure on costs and introduction of re-engineering, the size of HR functions was reversed with delegation to the line of many HR activities.

There are two key separate issues when we look at the developing role of HR in the future.

The first concerns how you organise HR and who should do what. Cost pressures and the impact of IT has caused many companies to pursue two alternative organisational forms: delegating the issues to the line and introducing business process re-engineering to the function. The two obvious solutions to the latter have been to segment the HR function into process-driven roles unrelated to the structure and/or to outsource generalist functions to another provider. The momentum behind these changes is accelerating and no HR function in future can ignore such developments.

Delegating to the line is often disliked by both HR specialists, who feel the loss of their craft, and line managers, who feel overloaded. Segmenting HR roles by process rather than function is disliked by managers who value accountability for departmental results. Outsourcing comes in for criticism where there is a gap between delivery and contribution to HR strategy.

The second issue concerns the essential contribution of HR and the core issue for this book; it is largely unrelated to these competing structural forms, even though at the moment structure and delivery holds centre stage. It is about the relationship between HR strategy and business strategy. An example of where HR and the line should be debating which strategy to follow relates to talent management.

Some would say that the crucial role for HR in the twenty-first century is managing talent in organisations, since finding, attracting, motivating and retaining talent is seen as the key limiting factor for agile organisations (see Chapter 9). In which case maybe Bruce Tulgan is right when he challenges managers in *Winning the Talent Wars* (Norton 2001) to 'turn your HR department into a strategic staffing war room'. The image reminds me of where I started – in a 'war room' dealing with the cut and thrust of IR in the 1960s and 1970s. Maybe it is plus ça change after all! HR with attitude.

There is plenty of room for debate, however. On the side of Bruce Tulgan comes McKinsey, who in their *Quarterly Report No. 2* (2001) say 'the war for management talent is intensifying dramatically'. In the blue (or is it red?) corner, on the other hand, Professor Jeffrey Pfeffer of Stanford University says the idea of a war for talent is dangerous nonsense – it militates against development of the whole organisation and knowledge-sharing by concentrating resources on an elite. Yet another view is provided in Chapter 7: maybe the strategic role of HR is situational and subject to context – to the life cycle of the organisation.

Summary

- There are three schools of thought on what preoccupies HR today: raising the function to the board (and beyond?) to show that HR can justify a position of equality with other functions; the 'hollowing out' of HR, with the function outsourcing or devolving to the line all activities other than HR strategy; no HR function at all – all managers should be people managers and the responsibility cannot reside in a single function.
- The role of the HR (or personnel) function in the 1960s and 1970s was to control industrial relations, which largely operated on an adversarial basis between workers and management. Set-piece collective bargains ruled the day.
- The 1980s saw the Thatcher administration tackling trade union power. HR was still on the fringe and change was driven by legislation, not from within.
- The mid-1980s brought an awareness of Japanese inward investment – a turning point for HR. Policy and strategy for HR became serious issues.
- The role of HR in the 1990s was to champion changes to culture and behaviour within the organisation to allow 'total quality' to be imported. This had to happen at every level: from boardroom to shop floor.
- HR in the twenty-first century is seeing a devolvement to line management. However, this trend is challenged by both HR professionals and line management – at least in the way that the model is applied.

References

1   RIDDERSTRALE J. *and* NORDSTRÖM K. (2000) *Funky Business.* London, FT.com.

2   MORTON C. (1979) *Collective Bargaining in Building and Civil Engineering.* Unpublished PhD thesis. London School of Economics.

3   *Ibid.*

4   MORTON C. (1998) *Beyond World Class.* Basingstoke, Macmillan. Reproduced with permission of Palgrave.

5   PATTERSON M. G., WEST M. A., LAWTHOM R. *and* NICKELL S. (1997) *The Impact of People Management Practices on Business Performance.* London, Institute of Personnel and Development.

Chapter 2

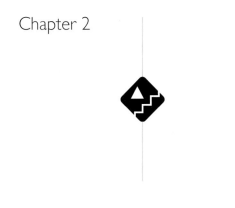

The challenge of sustainability in organisations

Clive Morton

The world of work has changed

We live in strange and interesting times. I was walking down Victoria Street in London recently when I became aware of a one-way conversation next to me. I turned expecting to see the usual – someone speaking animatedly into a mobile phone. To my surprise, it was an actual conversation between two people! What struck me immediately was that I should be surprised by a normal conversation. I have no doubt that this was a result of being in a busy city street where speed of travel and the stoic silence of commuters is de rigueur; however, it does show what we've become used to.

Speed of response today affects market share and profits. One month's lost development in Silicon Valley often means 70 per cent loss of market share for a new product.

In the 1980s, when the West was catching up with the quality movement (Japan as the exemplar), a business could argue that for competitive advantage only three measures of excellence were necessary to achieve distance from competitors:

◆ *quality* – highest quality of products and services
◆ *cost* – lowest cost in relation to quality
◆ *delivery* – on- or before-time delivery to customer satisfaction.

Today these three measures of excellence are qualification for market entry – not survival, let alone competitive advantage. Why? Because everybody is doing it. Hence the competitive advantage has to come from things like speed of response to customer needs.

The problem, though, is that speed of response is not wholly produced by systems or equipment. The vital ingredient is agility in companies and organisations. Agility is a function of culture and the degree of emotional commitment of the workforce. The ability to change culture is now the competitive advantage, since this provides the opportunity to give speed of the right sort of response.

The future world of work

Our thinking in the twenty-first century has been dominated by contrasts between new and old economies. The DTI Future Unit produced two scenarios in its 1999 report *Work in the Knowledge-Driven Economy*:

❖ *Wired world 'new economy'* comprises a network of economic agents coming together, via secure and efficient information and communication technologies (ICTs) on a project-by-project basis, held together by a web of contracts. Thus, self-employment and portfolio working are common, and small, innovative and responsive businesses have become the dominant force in the economy over large, established companies.

❖ *Built to last 'old economy'* starts from the basis that if knowledge is the principal source of competitive advantage, then it will be in the interest of business to capture and internalise that knowledge. This can be done by offering comprehensive remuneration packages to retain the individuals in whom knowledge is vested. Consequently, we see an economic landscape dominated by stable and often large companies, and extended families of companies. Self-employment and temporary contract work are therefore rare.

According to the report, a successful wired world is founded, amongst other things, on:

❖ the development of trust-based communications networks underpinned by strong personal and business networks. . .

❖ the creation of a culture and an economy in which individuals are willing and able to prosper outside the comfort zone of a stable company. . .

❖ the development of demand-led systems of learning that support individuals and their need for a complex mix of adaptable skills and competencies. . .

In contrast, the foundations for the built-to-last economy are:

- ❖ the use of comprehensive incentive packages designed to retain individuals within a company structure (for instance the development of education, share ownership, pension, healthcare and social benefits)
- ❖ the growing importance of brand in a truly global marketplace, with this brand forming a significant barrier to entry
- ❖ a utilisation of networking technologies and a culture of networking within companies and between stable groups of strategic partners to achieve competitive advantage.

The learning routines in new technology are directly opposite to the necessary attributes required for today's networked business – learning routines that appeal to the introverted mind when more and more the expanding network requires a high level of interpersonal skill and dependency on collaborative networks. However, both economies need trust, 'glue' and networks. This is a theme picked up throughout this book, and Jon and Andrew develop the argument in Chapters 3, 4, 6 and 8.

Operational excellence dominated the business ethos throughout the 1990s, creating massive changes in employment patterns. The dominant concerns in built-to-last companies were to continually drive down costs. It seemed as if ideas and entrepreneurial growth only existed latterly in the dot.com revolution or wired world.

Built-to-last companies found that costs went down, revenue went down, margins became thin or negative and morale was continually diagnosed as 'the lowest it's ever been'. HR professionals seemed to be fighting a rearguard action dealing with uncomfortable implementation and had no feeling of being able to influence strategy.

In the wired world, on the other hand, people were free to accelerate through their companies in a fraction of the time that their colleagues in the old economy could expect to progress. HR was not an issue. Money, share options and excitement were enough – until the bubble burst.

Built-to-last companies left the FTSE 100 list and then returned after dot.coms began to fail. Talent from the new economy had already started to migrate back to the old economy because of the more organised structural approach to career development.

<h2 style="text-align:center">‹to be sustainable you need trust, social glue and networks›</h2>

Talent management, as we will see, dominates today's HR agenda and has become a big issue in all organisations. The wired world has discovered that short-term excitement is not enough and the built-to-last world has found that it needs to become more agile. Both economies have become networked, creating new relationship patterns to manage. Despite the technology-dominated process models, managers have discovered that for the system to work and be sustainable you need trust, social glue and networks. Perversely, the technology can encourage more blunt and alienating language, straining ill-formed relationships.

Radical change in organisations – a key role for HR

Whether we focus on the old economy or the new economy, industry has had to cope with radical change. The most dominant link for HR into sustainability is one of change. Everyone will agree that change, rather than maintaining the status quo of the day, is the issue – in contrast to the examples from the 1960s and 1970s in Chapter 1. Andrew makes the point forcefully in Chapter 4 that to stand still is to go out of business.

How can HR help businesses and their people cope with change and how can they contribute to sustainability of business? This chapter answers this question by looking at the changes that both organisations and people have undergone in recent years (with a focus on the self-employed mindset, employability, and diversity and creativity).

I then look at how this happened, drawing some conclusions on competitiveness. This brings us to the key roles for HR (pre-empting some of Jon's thoughts in Chapter 3), namely:

- ❖ levers that HR can pull
- ❖ what is world class and what is the HR contribution?
- ❖ change in practice – Rolls-Royce and Anglian Water
- ❖ conclusions on change in organisations.

Finally, we need to bring it all together and focus on HR sustainability and its impact 'outside the factory gates'.

The first area is knowledge of how change can be effected in organisations. The HR professional will be faced with a wealth of definitive views. You change the people or you change the people. Many CEOs will have the view that you bring in new people – start afresh, no baggage. However, not all would agree with the wisdom of this.

Others will feel constrained either by history, law, trade unions or moral conscience not to push it – hence the extreme pressures from the RMT on London Underground to guarantee job security. The truth, as in most things, lies somewhere in between. Where on the spectrum the way forward resides can be down to the key contribution of the HR professional.

A parallel picture can be seen with the typical transition curve in change – it is very similar to the grieving process. William Bridges in *Managing Transitions* (1991) spoke of the transition curve and of how management could alter its depth and time span by positive intervention. Likewise the HR professional recognises that people have to *experience* a change process, not have it foisted upon them. Further than that the message from those who manage successful transitions is that the leaders have to *experience* the transition with their people, not at a distance from them.

It may be an old message, but the leaders, including HR, who can do the following are those who will inspire and energise the resultant workforce as the organisation comes out of its transition curve:

- ❖ recognise the grieving in change
- ❖ empathise and lament with those affected
- ❖ give space to think through new solutions
- ❖ be willing to listen and act on ideas from those affected.

This presents a new and formative role for HR professionals who want to make the difference. Jon talks of the HR director's role in being 'the employee champion' in Chapter 8 – this is a direct parallel to this message.

The new role is firstly informed by the experience of handling change in organisations. We now know that old arguments of a 'short, sharp shock' as opposed to phased implementation being better for organisations in transition (let alone for individuals) were based on fallacy and macho tendencies. There is strong evidence that leaders who turn a blind eye or distance themselves from the emotional turmoil of radical change are unable to inspire their people into new forms of business. The informed HR professional can guide and influence, support and encourage, but cannot do the job for all the other members of the management team.

The twenty-first-century organisation – totally networked

The modus operandi has moved from mass production, to decentralised production, to lean production, and now to agile production, characterised by the networked organisation. This applies whether it is in manufacturing, service or, increasingly, the public sector (see Figure 2).

Changes are not just a result of organisations reacting to external factors, thus moving from a hierarchical structure to a networked one. They are often led by rapidly changing individual expectations – not just from customers; employee perceptions have totally changed in the face of the loss of a job for life and the ease of job and career change. New phrases for this phenomenon are the 'self-employed mindset' or 'free workers' – we need to recognise that the attitudes of employees are different today.

Self-employed mindset

A study entitled *Tomorrow's People* by Professor Amin Rajan and Penny van Eupen (1997) – based on data from 350 organisations in the UK's financial, professional and business services sector –

Figure 2
CHANGES TO WORKING METHODS

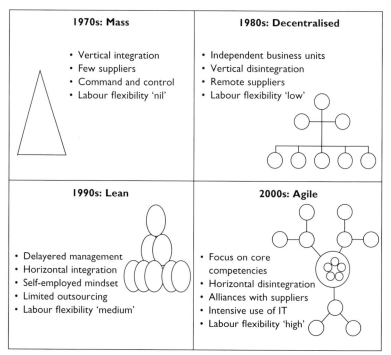

1970s: Mass	1980s: Decentralised
• Vertical integration • Few suppliers • Command and control • Labour flexibility 'nil'	• Independent business units • Vertical disintegration • Remote suppliers • Labour flexibility 'low'
1990s: Lean	**2000s: Agile**
• Delayered management • Horizontal integration • Self-employed mindset • Limited outsourcing • Labour flexibility 'medium'	• Focus on core competencies • Horizontal disintegration • Alliances with suppliers • Intensive use of IT • Labour flexibility 'high'

Source: Professor Amin Rajan, Create.

points out an important requirement from the workforce of today and tomorrow: mindset flexibility. This the authors describe as the 'self-employed mindset'.

At an individual level, the self-employed mindset is about coming to terms with three new facts of life about the employer–employee relationship.

First, the culture of a job for life has ended; however, many jobs still remain secure because *security is now based on performance, not paternalism.*

Second, to retain their jobs, staff have to:

❖ treat their employers as 'customers' of their labour services
❖ provide these services when and where they are needed

see themselves as *self-employed* persons keen to retain their customer's business

 be rewarded in accordance with their individual contribution

 acquire progressive skills that improve employability inside and outside their current organisations.

Third, although their employers will provide training towards acquiring progressive skills, *substantive responsibility for development will rest with the individual.*

This self-employed mindset occurs whether or not the context is 'permanent' full-time jobs, fixed-term contracts, temporary or part-time arrangements.

In the time since this report was published, the situation described has become fact in many more sectors of the economy. We need to recognise these changes and alter our approach to HR accordingly.

Employability

> ❛Job-seekers in the last decade have found that "soft skills" are just as important❜

The skills for employability in this new world have also changed. It used to be that having a trade, craft, technical skill or professional qualification was enough to guarantee an interview, and hopefully employment. Job-seekers in the last decade in developed economies have found that 'soft skills' are just as important. Recent studies on employability support these conclusions.

A 1999 study by the Centre for Research in Employment and Technology in Europe (with the Professional Development Foundation and supported by the CIPD) (ISBN 898879 230 and 257) found that the attributes needed for employability are a blend of:

 personal attributes that help to obtain a job in the first place

 soft skills that help to work with others in a changing environment

❖ practical skills that help to cope with change
❖ capabilities that help to stay ahead of change.

The researchers' view is that the current education system helps little with most of these areas, focused as it is on vocational and academic qualifications and obsessed with internal measures of performance.

Educationalists recognise the gap. The 1999 NACCCE report *All our Futures* on creativity, culture and education, jointly sponsored by David Blunkett and Chris Smith, concluded that there was 'a need for a much stronger emphasis on creative and cultural education and a new balance in teaching and in the curriculum. Over a number of years the balance of education has been lost. There is an urgent need to develop "human resources" and in particular to promote creativity, adaptability and better powers of communication.'

On the employability issue the report commented:

> We live in a fast-moving world. While employers continue to demand high academic standards, they also now want more. They want people who can adapt, see connections, innovate, communicate and work with others. This is true in many areas of work. The new knowledge-based economies in particular will increasingly depend on these abilities. Many businesses are paying for courses to promote creative abilities, to teach the skills and attitudes that are now essential for economic success but which our education system is not designed to promote.

Businesses too have had to change their focus away from solely using qualifications as means of selection. The mantra has been 'right people, right place'. They have had to look hard at both the personal attributes and the potential for creativity. The HR professional has been able to fill this measurement gap by the use of appropriate assessment. Richard Donkin in *Blood, Sweat and Tears* (Texere 2001) said of Henry Ford: '[He] created "component jobs" in that turning a screw on a moving assembly line could be an individual's sole job ... at the same time laying waste human potential on a massive scale.' It is only 30 years since militancy at Ford's Halewood plant in the UK was blamed on having intelligent people on the production line who were bored with the daily semi-automated grind. It is significant that in 2001 this plant will manufacture the new Jaguar X-Type, demonstrating the sea change in attitude and performance.

Diversity and creativity

Diversity used to be seen as an equal opportunity issue; at last the business case is clear – diversity leads to creativity, which leads to new business. Professors Jonas Ridderstrale and Kjell Nordström of the Stockholm School of Economics in their best-seller *Funky Business* write:

> $C = D^2$ where C stands for creativity and D for diversity. Lack of diversity often results in group-think and intellectual constipation. We all know what the others think, so what's the use in talking to them. From the point of view of innovation, opposites attract. Novelty is the result of constructive misfits and tension.

(See also Jon's comments in Chapter 3 on employing radical people from diverse backgrounds.)

This picture presents new challenges for management in focusing on sustainability. With a compliant workforce in a culture of command and control, management owned the total responsibility. Many were perfectly happy to accept orders – it came with the psychological contract. Keep your nose clean, don't rock the boat and you've got a job for life.

As soon as the quality movement encouraged individual responsibility and discouraged inspection of work, supervisors' roles changed. Now words like 'empowerment' crept in, along with a culture of 'support and stretch'. Previously only information and resources were required from management to get the job done. Now management had to gain what has since been called 'emotional commitment'. The old models of efficient communication didn't work. Management discovered there was a difference between understanding and energy. This meant a radical change in the way organisations needed to communicate. Understanding was not enough – it could breed a category of employees who went in for 'malicious obedience'. On the other hand, lots of

Figure 3
UNDERSTANDING/ENERGY CHANGE MODEL

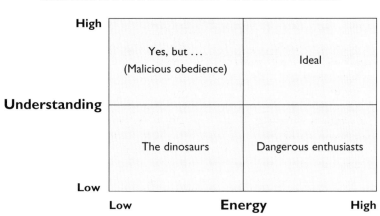

energy without understanding could lead to dangerous enthusiasm!

How did this transition from command and control to the need for high energy and understanding come about? Where does sustainability fit in? And where does HR have a role? I can trace the transition through my own experience in the last 15 years. Following the experiences mentioned in Chapter 1, a new phase opened up.

An encounter with lean production

I had the opportunity to set up the new Komatsu Plant in Birtley, Co. Durham, in 1986 – with the chance to change the approach to people management and productivity in manufacturing. Overall it was a great success. We benchmarked with the Japanese but did not copy (see Table 1). The solutions we found were British and suited a British workforce. Our customers, initially sceptical, became supportive of the UK product. The mould of UK manufacturing was broken and we found innovative solutions to perennial problems.

Table 1 was the product of my first visit to Japan and followed the open-ended brief Tetsuya Katada, then managing director of

Table I
FACTORS FOR SUCCESS

Japan	UK agenda
Focus on company/group	Focus on individual
Lifetime employment system	Applicable?
Seniority system	Applicable?
Company unions	Single-union agreements
Single status	Single status/flexibility
Continuous development	Continuous development
Education and training	Education and training
	Reinforce role of supervision
Consensus	Communicate and involve
'Bottom-up' reaction	Develop teams
Total quality control	Total quality control

Komatsu Ltd, gave me. The left-hand column was the analysis of factors that led to success in Japanese manufacturing. The right-hand column was our consequent agenda for the UK, which was all about investing in the people we were to recruit off the dole (or unemployment register).

What were the benefits of investing in people?

The benefits were clear: high levels of productivity (comparable with Japan), low sickness rate, minimal absenteeism and negligible turnover of staff. In essence it vitally improved the bottom line and made the company competitive. People close to the business noticed the difference. We had suppliers who commented, 'We fish in the same labour pool as you do, but you seem to get a lot more out of your people – how do you do it?' The factory is still a success story some 15 years and 40,000 machines later.

Total quality control – Kaizen

This was the only system of people management insisted upon from Japan and we accepted it willingly. After all, it had seen such success in Japan, with its quirky history emanating from those two great practical US gurus Deming and Juran.

The Kaizen system of encouraging shop-floor workers to innovate in small steps was enormously attractive – releasing pent-up energy as it did. It occurred to me that it provided the balance between control and empowerment. The control for production came in the shape of the 'standard method' of assembly from which you could not deviate, whereas Kaizen encouraged the same people to join quality circles to think the unthinkable – self-managing changes to processes, methods and manning. It is the modern equivalent of Alexander making short work of the Gordian Knot.

The concerns for HR were not confined in Komatsu UK to the shop floor and other employees of the company. They extended to supply chain management and the wider community. This was the stuff of sustainability; it wasn't termed that then, nor did we talk of stakeholders, but the reality has been that the relationship foundations laid for that factory have sustained it in bad times as well as good.

Supply chain management

Suppliers found that Komatsu personnel visited their workplaces to help reduce their manufacturing costs, not their margins, and at no cost to themselves (see Figure 4). The partnership philosophy goes deeper than just cost-cutting.

Figure 4
SUPPLY CHAIN REDUCES CORE COSTS

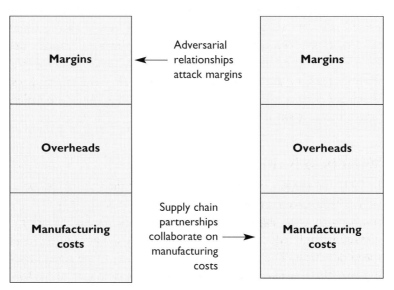

On one occasion a group of welders on the Komatsu production line had become frustrated about 'out of tolerance' parts from a supplier; they closed down production and travelled to the supplier's premises to enlighten their shop-floor workers as to what was needed. They succeeded where months of messages via the 'normal' channels had failed.

The wider community

HR was encouraged to take the lead in community involvement and relations. Employees were encouraged to become school governors, to get involved in charitable community projects and to bring their learning experiences back into work. It was there I discovered the real business case of what we now call CSR (corporate social responsibility). Employees would see how few resources charities manage on and use the examples to effect change within Komatsu.

In a strange way the adherence of the Japanese to teamwork between shop floor and office gave the biggest and most long-lived example of CSR. At the front of the site, a large office block lay redundant because office staff had been integrated with the shop floor. It had no planned use and was gradually deteriorating. I suggested to Tokyo that we could convert the block into a community project – perhaps a centre for those with disabilities. By providence the then UK government was encouraging joint public/private community projects. The Pinetree Centre was born. It still runs today as a one-stop shop for assessment, job-finding, training and business start-up for those with disabilities. It has set up over 200 successful businesses and aided countless others towards employment.

What help is this to HR?

In 1991 the market in Europe plummeted at the start of the recession. The situation arose that nobody thought would happen: the company that was expected to provide jobs for life had to face the inevitable and reduce labour costs. A great debate ensued over speed of action. The hawks argued for a short, sharp shock, feeling that the alternative was a slow, lingering death (or death by a thousand cuts). HR won the day with a phased reduction, over-time cutbacks and recruitment freezes – the usual short-term solutions – but the salvation was secondments (sometimes permanent) to other employers, charities and agencies based on the relationships built up on CSR. This softened the blow, gave career opportunities where they weren't obvious, and most importantly helped the morale within the factory.

HR needs to contradict the common myth put about by the hawks – that the retained workforce say 'good riddance' to those made redundant. They don't; they say, 'Will I be next?'

Conclusions on competitiveness

So, have the good ideas travelled? The short answer is yes. There is plentiful evidence that world-class practice is travelling and having competitive effect. This includes many of the lessons from Japanese manufacturing touched on above. The benchmarks taken by such global industries as motor manufacture are truly global – see the worldwide comparisons championed by Womack, Jones and Roos in *The Machine that Changed the World*. Those plants most closely associated with learning from Japan are at the top of the list in terms of productivity. However, even these world-class plants struggle against international currency obstacles such as the high-valued pound against the euro and other currencies. Commoditisation, overcapacity and the global nature of transactions and production mean that even world-class manufacturers cannot find a formula that is unalterable and sustainable.

Many companies have seen their fortunes disappear with amazing rapidity. Examples in manufacturing include Grove Coles, a crane maker for 150 years in the North East, which disappeared from view under intense competition from Europe and the Far East. Along with many other similar companies it has tried to learn the lessons of lean production – but that didn't save the company. This vignette can be repeated for many others: what caused Siemens to flee the North East eight months after opening a new £50 million silicon-chip-making plant? Similarly, was the demise of Rover under BMW ownership a result of poor productivity, the strong pound or inadequacies in the supply chain?

Productivity in the UK is seen to be some 30 per cent below the levels in Germany and 40 per cent below the USA. Recent events at Ford and Vauxhall, on top of the Rover/BMW experience, highlight the lack of competitiveness and show how fragile the UK manufacturing base is. A study by A. T. Kearney, *Future of the UK Automotive Industry*, published in May 2001, states that mass car production has no future in the UK because of the adverse effect of currency differences and the avowed intent of car manufacturers like Nissan, Honda and Toyota to shift parts sourcing to Continental Europe away from the UK. The manufacturers disagree, of course; however, the trend is downwards – overall production fell by over 10 per cent between April 2000 and April 2001 year on year.[1]

We should not assume that these issues are confined to the auto industry – it is merely the easiest worldwide industry to measure and to define individual country contributions. There is also the age-old argument concerning the value of manufacturing to the economy and whether decline of manufacturing in developed countries is inevitable and how much service industries can replace this decline.

‹ What do we do when the obvious solutions do not prevent decline and demise? ›

The issue for the HR contribution in relation to sustainability is what do we do when the obvious solutions (HRM, TQM, lean production and so on) do not prevent decline and demise?

Levers that HR can pull

Something that should be within HR's grasp to affect is employee satisfaction – but we don't seem to be doing well there either.

Professor Andrew Oswald at Warwick University has concluded from his recent study on job satisfaction in industry that the UK has one of the lowest scores – a staggering 64 per cent of UK workers get no satisfaction from their work. This contrasts with a high proportion of satisfied workers in Denmark (62 per cent), Switzerland (53 per cent), Spain (50 per cent) and the USA (49 per cent). Eastern European countries had the most disaffected workers, with only 23 per cent contented in Hungary, 27 per cent in Poland and 28 per cent in the Czech Republic.

The challenge is the same for the new knowledge-driven economy as the old asset-based economy. The assets for both are in the brains of employees, customers, suppliers and the community. Dot.com companies need satisfied, committed knowledge workers too!

What is world class and what is the HR contribution?

In 1994 I was introduced to a hierarchy of needs for a world-class company devised by James Maxmin, one of the many ex-CEOs of Laura Ashley. He has argued that many companies get stuck at the first rung of this ladder, concentrating on *operational excellence*. This is the stuff of business process re-engineering (BPR) but ends up as a qualification for market entry, not a differentiation with the competition. It can be seen as a convergent philosophy because all competitors will emulate it. Like the stuff of TQ – quality, cost and delivery – it can only give advantage over the competition for the time it takes for the others to catch up.

> What does world class demand?
> The company that is:
> – strategically led
> – competitively focused
> – market-oriented
> – employee-driven
> – operationally excellent

The four rungs above operationally excellent, according to Maxmin, can potentially add value for the aspiring world-class company (this is coincident with Professor Michael Porter's thesis that companies need to go beyond operational excellence to make strategic choices). It is interesting to note that independently

Andrew used the same model in his experience (see Chapter 5) but in a cyclical form, not a hierarchical ladder as in this case.

Experience of change at Rolls-Royce

In 1994 I moved to Rolls-Royce Industrial Power Group as personnel director. The organisation was focused on operational excellence and performance measures.

The problem was that this was what the competition was doing as well – there was no differentiation. Also, the total focus was on historical data – the gerbil wheel of the operations loop gave no prospect of seeing into the future or reframing strategy (see Figure 10 on page 41). We can see parallels to this in Andrew's and Jon's experience outlined in later chapters.

Progressively over the next two years efforts were made to share knowledge across the group – between the many subsidiaries that had previously been encouraged to look only vertically to the holdings board. This was to ensure that we would be more competitive and would build a shared vision. People systems were put in place to free up this knowledge-sharing. We used Peter Senge's *The Fifth Discipline* to introduce systems thinking, strategic positioning, personal mastery and shared vision, but complemented it with team profiling and interaction, transition management and guiding principles that were essentially about the 'soft glue' that

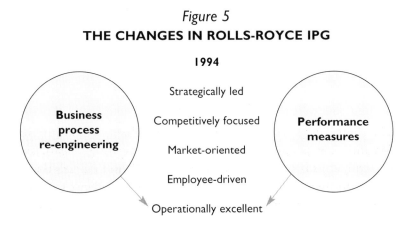

Figure 5
THE CHANGES IN ROLLS-ROYCE IPG

1994

Business process re-engineering

Strategically led

Competitively focused

Performance measures

Market-oriented

Employee-driven

Operationally excellent

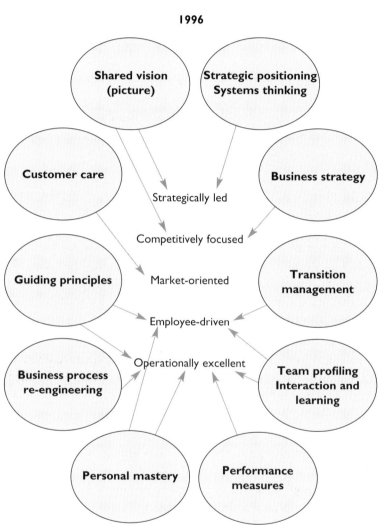

Figure 6
THE CHANGES AT ROLLS-ROYCE IPG

1996

joined the group together. This was an HR initiative that in the end changed business strategy – rather similar to Jon's experience of the value of soft glue in Chapter 3.

These processes were rather like a pincer movement, since the definition of soft glue and transition management operated at below board level, whereas the team profiling and interaction – the very key to change – operated first at holdings board level. It is interesting to note the parallels between this pincer movement example and the examples Jon and Andrew give in Chapters 3 and 4.

The nature of the business, with far-flung global interests, meant it was difficult to justify frequent board meetings. The result was that the board saw itself as a coalition and not a team. To work to become a team they needed to interact – otherwise, the concept of shared vision was unachievable.

On the back of failure in recruitment we started a process of personality profiling and assessment, which I was able to persuade my fellow board members would be useful for ourselves in our aspiration of developing as a team. The collective feedback on everybody's profiles at a board away-day represented a major culture shift. Team profiling was established; the board could see that they had been cloning themselves for years and that diversity was what was needed.

The use of Myers-Briggs Type Indicator and the decision analysis tool Action Profile became part of the language and was applied in subsidiary boards and teams as well.

The combination of 'freeing up' in the pincer movement fashion enabled radical change to take place at both subsidiary company level and the holding board of IPG. The focus was now on the 'reframing loop' of the learning board (see Figure 10 on page 41) as well as the operations loop that had previously dominated all board meetings. By 1996 the Rolls-Royce board were able to release themselves from the mindset of what had always been and dispose of unprofitable subsidiaries that had been seen as core businesses and unchallengeable. This is solid evidence of the contribution of HR to business strategy and the achievement of reaching 'strategically led' on the Maxmin hierarchy (see also Andrew's experience in Chapter 5).

Change in Anglian Water

It was time for me to move on again and I found a very different situation at Anglian Water. The company post-privatisation had made change a raison d'être. The board did not need persuading that radical change was necessary. The problem was that so much change had happened that initiative fatigue had set in. The expression 'initiativitis' stuck with a mood of resignation over new change programmes. 'Are we still doing TQ?', 'What happened to competency development?', 'Don't they know I've got a day job to do?'

This confusion deepened when the realisation sank in that many of the programmes were unrelated. With the beauty of hindsight I can see that these initiatives could be classified within three separate streams:

- process
- strategy
- people.

Figure 7 illustrates some of the programmes that had been initiated following privatisation. In 1996 there was fierce competition for

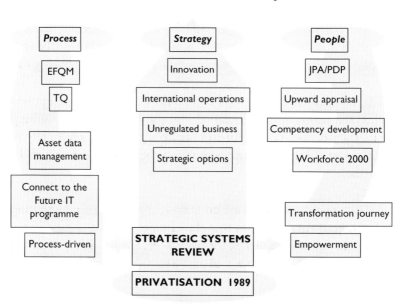

Figure 7
ANGLIAN'S TRANSFORMATION JOURNEY

attention, resources and time between the three streams and even within the streams. There were avid champions of any particular initiative bordering on the previous category of 'dangerous enthusiasm'. Often the separate streams had no relation to each other and the initiatives had been led by solutions imported into the organisation from outside.

**‹ It is all too easy to be attracted
to a packaged solution for which
a problem must be found ›**

This was a case, in retrospect, of a policy of adopting best practice and change for change's sake, not a policy of strategic intent. Regrettably such experience is not uncommon – it is all too easy to be attracted to a packaged solution for which a problem must be found. HR's role is often to take this issue back to fundamentals.

In order to bring some sense and understanding to this, I returned to Maxmin and plotted these initiatives against his hierarchy for a world-class company. My intention was to see whether these initiatives would lead to commercial goals – in particular, profit.

Frankly it turned out to be no more than a mapping exercise, but it did tell me that simply following the various constellations would not help the focus or the co-ordination needed for the step change (latterly termed Giant Leap) the company was looking for.

The solution that the new chief executive, Chris Mellor, applied after the previous strategy failed was essentially using a Deming quality tool, but one applied to business planning, not purely to Kaizen or continuous improvement at the production end of the business.

Policy deployment is based on the logic of telling and listening throughout the process so that the picture or policy is articulated from the top and the feedback from lower down the organisation leads to tuning the strategy objectives.

This gave the opportunity to both cascade and consult over the vision and values for the company before setting objectives for business units, teams and individuals. More importantly it gave the ability to focus on which initiatives directly added value and would lead to achieving Giant Leap and sustainability in the long term.

The resultant values, which are there today, are as follows:

- ❖ responsive
- ❖ responsible
- ❖ effective
- ❖ safe
- ❖ friendly
- ❖ competitive.

This focus on vision and values was only possible because of the work instigated in 1996 and 1997 on board, top team development and partnership with the trade unions. These were all HR-led initiatives, fully supported by the CEO. This developed a unity of purpose and alignment where the competition for attention between the earlier plethora of initiatives had failed.

We can now complete the diagram to show that it wasn't until vision and values had been established that the three streams could be brought together.

All current and new initiatives, together with behaviours by all participants, are measured against these values. The results are good. The first targets of Giant Leap have been met, with AWG being recognised as the foremost water and waste water company in the UK – an enormous improvement from being sixth only two years previously, and achieved two years before the target date of 2002.

The significant thing about these values is that they were already in the organisation – mostly before privatisation. The dialogue and openness that flowed from development and partnership enabled these values to be unearthed and used as a catalyst for progress. They are not just a unifying force; they give the key to sustainability.

Figure 8
ANGLIAN'S TRANSFORMATION JOURNEY

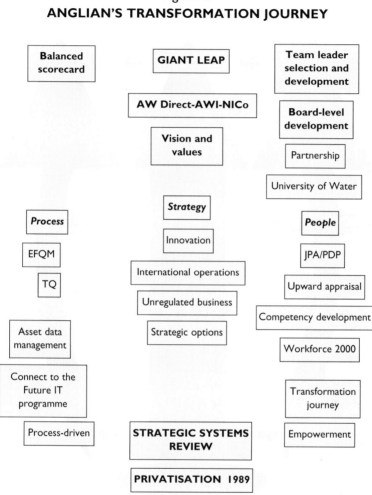

Not surprisingly the aspirations of the values had to be translated into very different competencies and behaviours within the company. The 'Boston matrix' in Figure 9 shows where learning and competence had to move from and to. AWG was a very professionally and technically based company and throughout this period had to shift via personal behaviour and business management to world-class leadership.

Figure 9

WHAT DID LEARNING AND COMPETENCE MEAN?
WHERE DID THEY NEED TO MOVE TO?

Business management	Leadership
The acumen to do AW's business profitably	The capabilities to lead AW's people and AW in its environment
Professional and technical	**Personal behaviour**
The knowledge and experience to produce AW's services and products	The range of interpersonal behaviour styles needed for AW's business culture

Conclusions on change in organisations

The key is cultural change. Chapter 4 reinforces this point, showing through experience that change cannot be forced on people and good long-term results be expected. Systems are helpful but will not be implemented without cultural change. Typically the culture has to shift from 'knowledge is power' (my knowledge ensures I have a job) to 'knowledge is shared' (I can grow because I share knowledge with others).

The question is how?

From the last 20 years of overseeing and leading transformation in organisations I am very clear:

Change is a process.

Change is about learning.

Change is not to be confined to the shop floor or coalface of operations. It has to be set from the top, with innovation set from the middle of the organisation.

The role of the board

Looking back on the Komatsu experience, we achieved great things from bottom-up change – the experience of change brought many visitors from across industry to seek change in their own businesses.

However, there was inevitably doubt in the minds of the visitors as to whether change could be effected in their organisations – doubt as to whether such change would be enthusiastically supported in the middle or even at the top of the organisation.

In moving on, as I did, to try to apply some of the learning from this experience in traditional UK industries, I found that getting change at the top became crucial. All the good work of Kaizen and innovation further down the organisation could be totally dissipated by negative behaviours and a lack of trust from the top.

I am clearer now: change must be set from the top; the board must be a learning board. Professor Bob Garratt in his seminal book *The Fish Rots from the Head* (HarperCollins 1996) uses the Chris Argyris model of double-loop learning to stress that the board needs to put equal weight on the reframing loop as on the operations loop (see Figure 10). This produces a third overlapping loop of the business brain.

The vast majority of boards put too much time and emphasis on the operations loop – this is the gerbil wheel of efficiency that has to go faster and faster and is based on overanalysis of historical data. At the

Figure 10
DOUBLE LOOP OF LEARNING

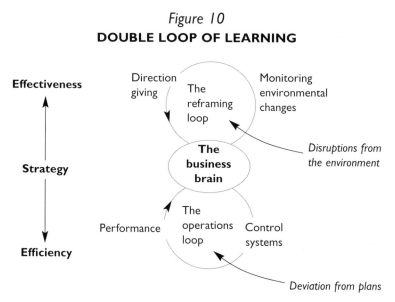

Source: Garratt B. (1996) *The Fish Rots from the Head.* London, HarperCollins.

same time they neglect the reframing loop, which is about effectiveness – matching the internal measures with signals from outside. This is another way that HR can contribute to the business – by being in touch with the world outside, understanding trends and influences.

A new role for middle management

Middle management is often the most neglected section of our industrial population. They have been progressively marginalised over the past two decades. The quality movement questioned their inspection role – did it add value? Empowerment in all its forms undermined supervisors' command and control, and flat organisations meant that the path to the top didn't have to pass through the middle management ranks after all. To add insult to injury, middle managers were downsized, rightsized or, as some say, capsized in the business process re-engineering exercises. Now they have lost professional HR support as migration to the line takes effect and middle managers willingly or unwillingly take on the specialist roles of HR.

'Middle managers can become the instigators of innovation in the centre of the organisation'

But there is another way. Middle managers can become the instigators of innovation in the centre of the organisation because they are at the interface between the aspirations of the top and the rough reality of operations.

Nonaka and Takeuchi, two Japanese academics who wrote *The Knowledge-Creating Company*, have termed the process 'middle-up-down management', which encapsulates the continuous interactive process of knowledge creation. It does require, however, a considerable degree of trust in middle managers by the top of the organisation – allowing them to form improvement teams, exploring possible innovations in processes or products – and listening and acting on the end result!

HR can help facilitate this process in terms of encouragement, training and empowering the organisation to think laterally and share knowledge.

Figure 11
MIDDLE-UP-DOWN KNOWLEDGE-CREATION PROCESS

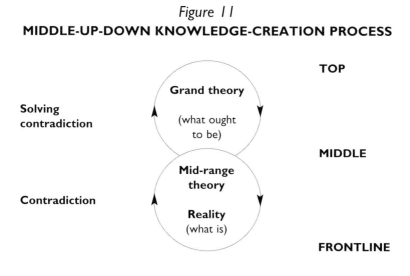

Bringing it all together

The leadership and decisive role for HR in organisations is becoming clear. The examples given by Andrew and Jon in this book demonstrate making *the* difference in terms of business viability. It is clear that none of the examples quoted ignores the social and economic environment that surrounds and interacts with the enterprise. Whether we subscribe to stakeholder theory or not, including all the stakeholders is as much HR's business as that of the CEO.

The benefits of HR being proactive in this area are legion:

 learning through the supply chain and through benchmarking globally (see the Allied Domecq examples in Chapter 4)

 being sensitive to the environment (ecological, social and economic) not only prevents adverse pressures but can also lead to new business (see reference to business development at Anglian Water)

 consumer groups can bring positive results; Komatsu often asks customers what they want in their next model when the latest is launched

❖ diversity and creativity in intellectual capital; we now know that 70 per cent of company assets are in the brains of employees, customers, suppliers – Generics practise this knowledge in its recruitment, development and spin-out policies (see Chapter 3)

❖ we need to accept and take advantage of the trend in all stakeholder groups of the 'death of deference' and the increasing ability to challenge; HR has an ethical role in promoting transparency, openness and good corporate governance for sustainability

❖ leadership is about dealing with dilemmas, shades of grey, issues of complexity, not black and white simple formulae.

Collins and Porras in *Built to Last* demonstrated that success was not about choosing an extreme – business had to balance short- *and* long-term pressures and so not choose one or the other. HR can help with this by understanding and anticipating the views of stakeholder groups and factoring this into business strategy. The people contribution is then achieved by the development that can follow – the understanding of the nature of leadership right down the organisation – right away from dependence on one person's black and white vision.

Getting out of the office

The polemic is that businesses should achieve partnerships with their stakeholders for their own good and the stability and growth of society. If it is of such obvious benefit, why doesn't it happen as a rule?

❖ a mistaken impression that to focus on stakeholders other than shareholders waters down focus on profit

❖ involvement outside the firm looks like escapism, or opting out

❖ it looks like inviting in more complexity to an already complex world – however, examples in Chapter 3 from Jon's experience show that it helps resolve complexity.

The truth is that it is proven that partnership gives longevity to the organisation, learning about the business, social and natural environment and the licence to operate. Such an investment of time pays off to the individual, the organisation and the community.

I have a beautiful example from my time at Anglian Water. The transformation journey, in full swing when I joined in 1996, was consistently criticised by my peer group as not attacking bottom-line costs. It seemed that all the 'journey' groups of employees were keen to do things in the community. This was regarded by my peers as a waste. Four years later AWG has a viable subsidiary selling non-water products to its 6 million customers in the UK. This was established after a market survey showed that customers trusted AWG because of the work done in the community. Companies never know when business benefit arrives because of a proactive stakeholder approach, but the evidence is that it will deliver. Similar evidence can be seen in Chapters 3, 6 and 9 from Jon's and Andrew's experience.

Bringing all the forces together to produce sustainability[2]

The Centre for Tomorrow's Company has shown that those companies that are *inclusive* in their relationships inside and with their communities stay the course, are consistently more profitable and more able to make strategic choices for the future. We know that individuals need organisations in which to develop and that communities need both companies and people to contribute for mutual benefit. Organisations benefit from being active in the community and HR needs to champion such policies. Looked at deeply, HR can see that its own strategies can benefit from linking with and supporting CSR policies.

The challenge for HR today is to recast the role that will give the best contribution to the sustainability of their organisation.

Summary

 People are the competitive advantage. Excellence in cost, quality and delivery have become requirements for entry into a market, not success within it. Speed of response to the customer requires an agile organisation based on the emotional commitment of the workforce.

 The HR function must take the lead in change if the business is to be sustainable. This goes beyond an appreciation of the various 'expert views' to an understanding of your particular organisation, its market and competitors and, most importantly, the employees (from the board to the shop floor).

- The nature of the employment relationship has changed – the emergence of the self-employed mindset and a shift in the skills required by employers towards interpersonal skills. Empowerment has its own impact upon sustainability.
- Japanese principles on quality that were adopted throughout the 1980s and 1990s have brought with them key lessons in people management. These are relevant regardless of the organisation's area of business.
- Beware best practice and change for change's sake. Both have their undeniable place in the HR professional's toolkit, but there must be a valid need for their use.
- Don't rush to graft ideal values onto the organisation. Open communication and partnership can often lead to the emergence of key values that are already within the organisation. These values then become a unifying force.
- HR has a key role to play in acting as the conduit between internal organisational factors and outside trends and influences.
- Consideration must be given to middle management, which is increasingly expected to take on HR roles as migration to the line gathers pace.

References

1   BURT T. *and* GRIFFITHS J. (2001) 'Report warns of end for volume car assembly'. *Financial Times*. 24 May. p2.

2   MORTON C. (1998) *Beyond World Class*. Basingstoke, Macmillan. Reproduced with permission of Palgrave.

Chapter 3

What is the role of HR today?

Jon Sparkes

A question of credibility?

This chapter is about the credibility of HR people. The role of HR today is varied, both horizontally across a range of activities, and vertically, from the firm administrative base through to leadership in the strategy process. Without credibility, the role of HR is limited and often self-limiting. Credibility is not simply about being a business partner; it is this and much more.

The chapter is also the first step towards describing how HR can change itself, and also lead and contribute to the sustainability of organisations. In Chapter 2, Clive Morton described many of the issues facing organisations today and many of the tools we have tried and are trying to ensure that organisations can develop and change in a world that is itself changing more rapidly and more radically than ever before. It's a small example, but I am typing this somewhere over the Atlantic as I head out to visit a recently acquired company in Baltimore. This ability to work from a lightweight laptop while in transit from the UK to the USA is barely radical nowadays, but was unheard of less than a handful of years ago. Not only will I complete the chapter during the flight, but I will e-mail it to Clive and Andrew as well as our editor. Having e-mailed this, I will respond to all of my correspondence from the comfort of my Baltimore hotel room. By the time my colleagues get in to work tomorrow morning it will be as if I had been there all the time.

I have been fortunate enough to work alongside some fantastic human resources professionals in a variety of situations. Wherever I have observed HR professionals I have admired, I have seen them surging towards the position of business partner. Business partner has meant several things, but essentially has been about contributing to the success of the business and being clearly recognised for such contribution.

These people, whom I describe as fantastic HR professionals, have all demonstrated a common set of capabilities. Among many positive attributes, there are four I would point to as being key:

- ❖ a depth of understanding of their business context
- ❖ exceptional analytical skills
- ❖ a highly developed political and diplomatic capability
- ❖ the sensitivity and insight required to deal with intense and complex interpersonal situations.

I would argue that although this set of capabilities is not common across organisations, using it is nonetheless now at the heart of HR's role. The role has evolved, and we are left with an often complex, challenging and rewarding position in the network organisations of today. We have been welfare officer, administration manager, employee services function, industrial relations technician and chief negotiator, staff development co-ordinator, expatriate support manager, compensation and benefits professional, and many, many other things.

In the early to mid-1990s we became the human resources department and espoused HRM, positioning ourselves with the key business techniques of the day – TQM, BPR, MRP, metrics, benchmarking, downsizing, employee participation and so on. More recently, we have become a chartered profession.

Along the way, we have established a unique toolkit for contributing to business success through the development, reward, motivation, organisation of and concern for people. But there is a risk. The risk is that the human resources profession has achieved a unique set of capabilities and could commit the great HR sin of failing to fulfil its potential! Without a clear view of our role and how to achieve our objectives, this set of HR skills will go to waste.

So, what is the HR role today? What do we have to do to convert our day-to-day efforts into organisational success, a motivated workforce and fulfilling careers?

This chapter will begin to answer these questions by:

- ❖ defining a framework based around a very simple analogy that summarises the vertical and horizontal complexity of the HR role
- ❖ emphasising the need for credibility among the stakeholders of HR
- ❖ sketching out an image of what it means to be a business partner.

I will illustrate many of my points through experiences at the Generics Group, a company that I have been involved with for almost six years. It clearly demonstrates the move to network organisation and the recognition of the crucial asset of knowledge workers. I have been with the company through both significant growth and the move from private company to public listing, giving me the opportunity to see strategy and organisational development hand-in-hand with the development of the HR function.

Soft glue

HR today provides both lubrication and glue to assist the organisation in working smoothly and effectively, without undue friction, at the same time as providing cohesiveness at an organisational and personal level. Or, as Bahrami and Evans[1] put it:

> The HR team has to create and manage the soft glue which not only binds and aligns, but also motivates.

This observation by Bahrami and Evans is based on a study of many knowledge-based, sophisticated technology companies, including a number in Silicon Valley. The study emphasises the element of the present in the question of the role of HR today.

Organisations today are different, and it is the nature of today's organisation that helps shape the role of HR today.

‹ HR can no longer rely on the tried and tested solutions to organisational and personnel issues ›

Modern businesses and organisations are becoming less formal and structured and more like (sometimes chaotic) networks – something biological or biochemical more than mechanical and deterministic. There is a growing recognition that you cannot formulate a fixed set of inputs to create a fixed set of outcomes, and indeed that small variations in input will result in large and relatively unpredictable variations in output. HR can no longer rely on the tried and tested solutions to organisational and personnel issues, problems and challenges.

Knowledge-based organisations and the knowledge workers populating them have different needs from the once more common process-, product- or service-driven businesses. Knowledge organisations need innovation, creativity and solutions to insoluble problems. Knowledge workers need superb colleagues, freedom and self-determination, challenging and interesting work, a working environment that positively enhances their experience of work, and the favourable interplay of that experience with their lives outside work.

Of course, my reference to knowledge-based organisations must be seen in its broadest sense. This is not just the small and medium-sized high-technology companies of the silicon valleys, glens, fens and clusters. All organisations today can be seen as knowledge-based. Certainly, my experience in a large telecommunications manufacturing company would support this argument. In that company 10 years ago, we were working on the premise that it was the knowledge and interactions of the employees that held the key to a more successful business. There were many examples of developing systems and processes that enabled the company to draw on the full knowledge and talent of the employees, from the introduction of innovation schemes, the development of early broadbanding grading structures, and the move from production line to U-Cell manufacturing. The HR department played a leading role in many of the innovations in this company.

Little wonder we cannot describe the role of HR today in traditional terms like welfare, resourcing, industrial relations or employee services. It is a networked role in the 'agile organisation', described by Clive Morton in Chapter 2. It is helping the organisation to achieve its aims through a combination of freeing up and slowing down. The key to credibility is knowing when to speed things up and when to slow things down.

As we move forward, we should keep in mind the analogy of simultaneously enabling the smooth, frictionless running of the organisation and applying the necessary glue to achieve cohesion and connectivity.

Getting HR credible

Thus far it has been important to start to understand the context of today's human resources professional, building on some of Clive's comments in the earlier chapters. Now we must seek the beginnings of a more tangible description of the role as played out by tens or hundreds of thousands of HR people every day.

The role of HR might be seen as irrelevant unless the HR function is credible. There are two aspects of getting credible:

 being credible
 being seen to be credible.

The HR function (or the individual HR professional) can control both aspects to a greater or lesser degree. It can certainly control the first, and it should not be so fatalistic as to think the second is out of its hands.

This credibility factor is described by Wayne Brockbank[2] in the following way:

Before strategic HR agendas can be brought to the strategy table, senior management has to perceive that HR has 'earned a place at the table'. Earning that place at the table is a function of many factors, including the following: knowing the strategy, culture, vocabulary, and operating systems of the business; having passion for issues which add greatest value to external customers and shareholders; and focusing on financial results.

This is applicable whether we are talking about strategic human resources or the day-to-day provision of HR services. So what must the HR function, or the individual HR professional, do in order to start to become credible?

Delivering the support service

It is tempting to start from the so-called top and describe HR's credibility and role in terms of strategic leadership and delivery of corporate strategy. However, credibility starts in a completely different place.

The administrative function of HR is essential. In our efforts to become business partners, we forget the administrative function at our peril. We may outsource it or find some other innovative way of removing it from the day-to-day advisory and management activities of HR, but it must be delivered. If someone receives a letter confirming their new salary and it is wrong, then we have taken several steps back in fulfilling our role in the organisation and achieving business partner status. There are several other areas we might neglect to leave us time to concentrate on being business partners:

❖ *Data collection and administrative rigour* – when my current company was preparing to float on the London Stock Exchange, we were able to benefit from what had often seemed like unnecessary and petty administration – the collection of copies of the certificates of new recruits. Having described ourselves to the market as employing highly qualified people, we then needed to support this with numbers and were able to audit-trail back to the BSc, BA, MBA and PhD certificates of our people.

❖ *Welfare* – this has been and remains an essential element of the HR portfolio of activities. We are correct in training managers to deal with welfare issues and we are right to draw on and signpost to external support services. However, we would be failing if we left it at that. The cost to the company of an individual sinking below the weight of personal problems can be easily calculated and it is crucial that HR gets involved as appropriate. The best place for dealing with such difficulties is either with the local manager or with an external professional support service, but HR should get involved by at least providing a link between these two aspects of the process – and, if needed, by working with the individual directly (but only if personally qualified to do so).

✥ *Secretariat* – many HR colleagues will hate to see me including this in a description of the role of HR today. However, who better to take the minutes of the remuneration committee meeting than the HR director? This is something many more HR professionals would aspire to rather than dismiss as administration. Who better to spend hours, days and weeks going through the laborious paper-pushing process of granting share options to the entire company than the HR function? If we deliver these support services effectively, we have much to gain as a profession and much to gain within our organisations.

I cannot overplay the importance of the delivery of the support service; it is the foundation on which we build an effective and credible HR function. We must find ways of ensuring the cost-effectiveness and the efficiency of the processes involved, but we mustn't deny their importance.

However, we must not do these things just because they've always been done that way: there must be a business case. In my current organisation, innovation is everything. We follow some of the principles we were all taught in secondary school science, and in particular that, as innovation often happens at the interface between disciplines, we should seek to maximise the interactions between people. All of a sudden some of the items those who espouse 'strategic' HR have hidden away from have come to the fore. We look at the staff canteen in a different light – somewhere to feed people, or somewhere for people to mix? We determine policy on homeworking at a time when we are short of space in what may seem a counterintuitive fashion – what's more important, lack of space or innovation? For the networked organisation, the knowledge-based organisation and the innovation-dependent organisation, suddenly the things we tried to let go of as we moved from personnel to HRM are coming back into vogue!

For example, my team manages HR for several businesses as a result of our policy of creating and developing new spin-out companies. This can be a frustrating process because to some extent these businesses are competing in the employment market. As a matter of policy we run recruitment supply chains with a fair degree of independence, for the conflict of interests inherent in receiving a superb CV for an electronics design engineer is unnecessary. However, while avoiding the conflict, we must also benefit from the synergy. The role of the individual who diligently logs the arrival of CVs and tracks their progress becomes essential.

The role is also crucial in ensuring high-speed turnaround of CVs, as speed is often of the essence. When you come late to the game and offer a job to an individual with six offers already 'in the bag', you appreciate the need for rapid turnaround. The diligent tracking of CVs and chasing managers for decisions clearly adds value to the company and has a direct impact on the revenue line of the accounts.

Deliver on promises

‹Where we don't succeed, we must understand why we didn't›

One of my recent challenges has been the achievement of steep organic growth targets. The delivery of such promises starts with the establishment of the necessary resources to deliver the promise – easier said than done, maybe, and something of a chicken-and-egg situation in terms of credibility of the HR function. The HR function and individual HR professionals cannot afford to shrug their shoulders and accept anything less than full delivery of promises. Where we don't succeed, we must understand why we didn't and have new answers for how we will in the future.

Recruitment is no longer about selecting the best people; it is at the heart of the so-called talent war. We must follow every lead and try every new approach in order to deliver on our promise to grow and develop the business. There was a time when recruitment campaigns followed the textbook approach:

❖ Consider whether recruitment is necessary.
❖ Draw up the job description.
❖ Define the person specification.
❖ Agree on whether to advertise internally or externally.
❖ Advertise and await response.

This is of course the right way to run the process, but no one ever delivered a promise like that. For Generics, recruitment is about adding even more brilliant people to an organisation already brimming with brilliant people. It is about building a level of intellectual capital second to none in order to deliver effective and radical solutions to our clients, generate highly valuable intellectual property and create new companies that will add exponentially to the value of our business. It is about making the work experience of existing employees even more fulfilling by adding even more exceptional colleagues with even more new and different capabilities.

So we cannot sit back and hope that the recruits will come in; that would be to have failed before we've even started. It is of course different for every organisation. However, the approach we have adopted borrows much from the principles of supply-chain management:

❖ by involving everyone in the organisation in the process
❖ by careful and proud management and protection of our brand in the employment market
❖ by recognising the importance of our suppliers and treating them with due respect.

Involving everyone in the organisation may seem like a glib statement. In its most tangible form, this is the financial *bounty* payment we make where people are instrumental in identifying a suitable candidate, procuring their CV and developing their interest in the company. Beyond that we run a recruitment pipeline that involves secretaries from across the organisation as the co-ordinators of first meetings with candidates, the most appropriate person in the company as screener of the CV, managers as the champions of candidates moving towards offer stage, receptionists as the key first impression of the company, anyone with the relevant skills as interviewers, and our CEO meets almost every candidate before we make an offer. Everyone in the organisation recognises the importance of recruiting and everyone plays a part in recruiting.

Careful and proud management and protection of the brand should also permeate every individual in the company. This goes far deeper than proper training and briefing of interviewers. Quick and correct decisions must be made, a significant amount of contact time for candidates should be allowed, with a minimum of two hours' contact time for a first interview, leading to a total of eight or more hours' contact time when the company is particularly keen to get someone on board. The experience for the individual has to be wholly positive regardless of outcome.

Looking outward is an important aspect of managing the brand. HR works very closely with the team responsible for the website to ensure that recruiting is emphasised and that other aspects of the site help send an accurate message about the organisation. We show a great deal of willing in working with journalists and other people with an interest in the business. We spend as much time as possible showing recruitment agents the insides of the business. Crucially, the 'we' I refer to is not just HR, but all of the recruiting managers in the organisation – led and co-ordinated by HR but, as discussed, recruitment has become a key element of everyday working for many people across the company.

Finally, the recognition of our portfolio of suppliers is very important. There are many things we must do to develop, protect and nurture our relationships with such people and organisations. Just as I would never expect a supplier to put an unsolicited CV on the fax, we will not simply put a job specification on a fax and send it to an agent without the reciprocal level of relationship-building.

So delivering against promises is crucial. Hopefully this example demonstrates that HR must not and cannot afford to take a fatalistic view of this. We must constantly strive to find new, radical approaches to delivering promises. HR cannot just hope for the best – it would be wholly unacceptable for any other business function to do this, so why should we?

Leadership on key HR matters

This is about leadership on home territory issues. It goes without saying that HR should take the lead of key HR issues. However, I have seen organisations where HR takes far from a leading role, even on these issues.

I will use the example of career development to demonstrate how HR must take the lead, either from the front or through forcing the pace where there is clear joint responsibility.

Generics, like many organisations today, has a non-hierarchical approach to business. That is not to say it has no hierarchy, because there certainly is an appropriate level of structure. However, it is the behaviour that is crucial. Anyone in the company could quite feasibly find themselves reporting to anyone else in the company in the context of a client project or an internal project. This flattens hierarchy without endangering the effectiveness of decision-making and leadership.

In such a flat organisation, career development becomes difficult to see. Having reached this conclusion in an organisation, several things might happen:

- the fatalistic shrugging of shoulders mentioned earlier and the laissez-faire approach that places responsibility for career development in the lap of the individual
- fragmentation as various enlightened areas of the business build their own career development approach
- unnecessary and inefficient building of hierarchy by creating management roles into which people can be promoted
- centralised initiatives to impose a prescribed competency framework on the business.

Each approach has its merits. We took a slightly different approach. Led by HR, but involving a number of people from across the business, we started to consider how we might build a career development approach for the consultants (representing about 70 per cent of the company's population).

This approach involves identifying a small number of people who will be recognised by anyone as having developed their career in the company, and working backwards from there. This is a simple approach, but relatively novel in the attitude if not in the mechanics. Look at the aims of the business as a sanity-check on tracking the careers of individuals rather than constructing something top-down.

The output is simply known as a Career Grid. The nearest analogy I can find is that of the output display for a graphic equaliser. This is not a competency framework where everyone strives to get to the top in as many areas as possible. It is a career planning tool, where people can take a portfolio approach to their career. They can decide that in order to achieve their aim to move forward in business management they actually need to divert some of their efforts from the achievement of technical guru status into project management and business development or selling. They may decide that in order to satisfy their career aspirations in innovation or innovation exploitation they ought to take a step back in their efforts to manage every project coming their way.

The role of HR in career development – one of the most critical of HR matters – is to:

- recognise the importance of an issue to individuals and company alike
- take immediate responsibility for finding the solution
- ensure that the solution is appropriate and that the process for identifying and achieving a solution is appropriate given the cultural and structural context of the business
- lead but not necessarily dominate the process
- identify and involve the full range of stakeholders in specification and design phases if you wish to achieve any semblance of buy-in at implementation phase

❖ close the loop by ensuring that your employee surveys enable feedback on the process in question.

This may be a definition of leadership. The point is that the company's agenda and the agenda of employees are combined to produce something useful to all stakeholders. The catalyst for change and the leader of change is not the HR textbook but an appropriate form of leadership on the part of the HR professional.

So a significant part of the role of HR today is leadership on key HR matters. However, this is not dogmatic leadership but leadership from within the management team, and leadership with consultation and a clear understanding of the business context.

Custodian of culture and change

This is an issue developed by Andrew Newall in the next chapter. However, a description of the role of HR would not be complete without considering the question of culture and change. In my current role, culture is crucial. Indeed the prospectus which heralded the flotation of the company pointed directly at culture as a key factor in the company's value proposition.

In this example, it is clear that while the company aims to grow, it is also important to retain a culture that supports, nurtures and promotes innovation. Here I will draw on the '$C = D^2$' formula from Chapter 2 relating to creativity and diversity. Our aim is to ensure not only that the company can continue to innovate as it grows, but that the increased rate of innovation can outstrip the rate of headcount growth. Employing radical people from a diverse set of backgrounds can only help this, and the steadfastness of the organisation to retain a culture that underpins innovation and creativity must also help.

> ‘The failure of change is usually the failure to achieve the right culture’

The role of HR in culture and change is essential. Change fails unless the people and implementation aspects are dealt with early on. This point is clearly demonstrated by Andrew in the next chapter. The failure of change is usually the failure to achieve the right culture for the right business circumstances.

Clear understanding of the business

This might be seen simply as a means to an end. As discussed earlier, in providing leadership on HR matters, a clear understanding of the business context is important. However, the role of HR today goes beyond just using an understanding of the business to do HR things.

HR has a significant role to play in communicating business strategy and in demonstrating the culture of the organisation. Having a clear understanding of the business is now becoming a part of the role, not just a competency that enables us to do our jobs better.

For example, Generics has a strategy for commercialising technology through the spin-out of new companies. There are many good reasons for doing this, and indeed we are now able to draw on the experience we have to deliver consulting assignments that enable other companies to do the same. Incubation and spin-out is becoming big business for big businesses.

This strategy:

- ❖ enables intellectual property to reach the market rapidly
- ❖ enables early leverage of external funding for potentially very valuable businesses
- ❖ provides unique career opportunities for creative, entrepreneurial employees
- ❖ allows the delivery of great value to the stakeholders.

A couple of years ago it became clear that internal and external observers alike would benefit from a guide to the principles of spin-out. This was not to be a blueprint, because each one is different. I worked to develop an appropriate level of codification for the process to ensure a clear view of why spin-out was advantageous to business and individual alike. This codification became a booklet which has been useful internally and externally to explain this complex aspect of the company's business model.

This was seen as naturally being a job for the head of HR. In other businesses it might not have been so. However, I have observed similar examples elsewhere – the creation of an organisational development function in a large engineering company, situated within the HR function and led by an HR person, but with responsibility for engineering and manufacturing process improvement as well as more traditional people development functions. That HR person went on to become the quality director, a great example of an HR person moving into a crucial operational role – something we see too little of.

The message is that demonstrating an understanding of the business is no longer just a tool of the HR professional's trade: it is part of the job now.

Challenge and support the line

During the mid-1990s customer services vogue, a paradox in the HR role became very clear. At that time everything that moved had customer service metrics attached to it. I had several disagreements at the time with those responsible for implementing customer service initiatives about the applicability in HR.

My earlier comments on providing the support service demonstrate clearly that we must provide high levels of customer service, so clearly we must benchmark ourselves in this area and encourage our customers to measure our service levels. Indeed in many cases, sheer size of organisation is leading us to a call centre approach for HR policy advice. The need for service-level agreements and clear metrics for customer service in such circumstances is paramount.

The role of HR today, among other aspects, has got to be adding value to the line. We have to be able to clearly see how we have enhanced the ability of operational managers and directors to deliver the aims of the company. This is essentially about supporting them through the development and delivery of policies for resourcing, retention, motivation, development and reward. We have to respect the decisions and plans of operational managers and move the whole raft of HR interventions in behind those decisions and plans.

The paradox becomes clear at the point of challenge. The role of HR today is not simply one of supporting: it is also about challenging the line – and how do you put a customer service metric on that?

When my team supports the growth of the business through effective recruitment processes, it is very clear that we are providing support to our customer. When we negotiate and challenge the operational director to push more resource into recruiting, this takes us beyond simply supporting.

When HR provides a transparent and objective means for determining salary, which ensures internal consistency and enables managers to be confident in the integrity of their decisions, the support for our customers is clear. When we push the external market element of compensation and benefits, and threaten the operating division's bottom line and margins by insisting that we pay a new employee an anomalous salary, then which operational manager is going to feel supported and give us 100 per cent for customer service?

When a manager expresses a stereotyped view about a particular group of people, do we follow a policy of the customer is always right or do we challenge the statement and, in the extreme, instigate disciplinary procedures? What will these approaches do for the relationship with the customer?

The answer is of course to understand who the customer is. For HR, the customer is the whole portfolio of stakeholders. It is the CEO and the managers and the individual employees and potential future employees. It is the suppliers and it is the shareholders. It is the individual sales manager and it is the people in the local community. Ultimately the deliverable from HR is something that supports the achievement of business aims in the short, medium and long term. We do ourselves no favours as HR professionals or members of the management team if we simply support the short-term goals of the managers.

It is the role of HR today to challenge the line. This is not always comfortable, isn't the best approach to making friends and is never easy, but it is our job. In the long term, of course, we achieve more, satisfy the long-term needs of the business and probably make more real friends this way.

Resolve the gap issues

In every business there are issues that are nobody's responsibility and everybody's responsibility. The effective HR professional must be adept at taking these on board.

A classic example is health and safety. There are few honest HR professionals who relish the opportunity to take responsibility for health and safety. Compared to the cut and thrust of recruitment, the satisfaction of employee development or the intellectual challenge of the rewards portfolio, health and safety doesn't seem so attractive.

However, this is an area where we can contribute very well. Our understanding of the whole business and our willingness to challenge the line make us excellent candidates for this job. Not only that, but most HR professionals will also recognise a cultural lever when they see one, and in my organisation health and safety falls right on the interface between responsible risk management and the freedom of the individual. On joining Generics, I made it very clear that HR should at least be represented on the health and safety committee.

We have taken this a step further through the creation of a management group responsible for integration and synergy across business functions. I chair this group, which includes the finance director, group legal adviser, facilities manager, and the information and technology services manager. This is already bringing great benefits as the forum for resolving many *gap* issues, such as:

 confidentiality and security policy, encompassing terms of employment, terms of business, physical security, IT systems integrity, access to the building for clients and tenants

 e-mail traffic management and policies, where IT and HR are

able to work as one with on-tap advice on the legal complexities

✦ managing the integration of newly acquired businesses in a co-ordinated fashion across the IT and facilities integration and the cultural integration – simple things like the head of IT and the head of HR visiting the acquired company together with the dual objective of physical support and giving a sense of being welcomed by the new parent company.

HR has been able to provide both the glue and the lubrication to effective cross-function working. This may be an extreme case, and it is early days, but the principle applies elsewhere. The point is that part of the role of HR today is to make it their business to get involved in gap issues.

Getting out of the office

This element of the role sees HR out of their traditional internal support confines. Some in the line may see this as a dangerous move, but it is essential nonetheless: how can you manage HR without a view of the outside world? Here I'll draw on three reasons for looking outward, but I am sure there are many more.

First, there are good HR reasons for looking outward. The successful HR function should be tasked with ensuring the supply of excellent people to fuel the growth of the business. This is more than hiring people; it is about becoming the employer of choice. I look more closely at this in Chapter 9, but here I will point out a number of external issues we need to be involved in:

✦ *Employment market* – the employment market is a complex web of educational establishments, the ups and downs of similar organ-isations or organisations employing similar people, trends in the job-search methods of the people we need to develop the inno-vative heart of the business, recruitment agents, headhunters, friends of friends, and of course the large number of people who might be potential candidates. We cannot understand this market from the comfort of our office any more than a retailer can understand his or her market from behind the counter.

✦ *Society and government* – we need to understand what is hap-pening in the regulatory framework and the social context of our businesses. This is especially complex for those of us in international businesses. Again, this information doesn't just arrive on your desk; the HR professional has to go out and find it and influence it.

♦ *Competition* – we need to know what our competitors are doing, and they certainly won't just arrive at your office with the information you need. This must go beyond the salary surveys – as a senior director in a large Swiss company said to me recently, 'Salary surveys just tell you that everyone should get an above-average pay raise!' We must work to establish relationships with our competitors for mutual advantage, as well as gleaning the information from internal sources.

The second reason for getting out of the office is simply because we are acting as responsible members of our management teams. In a growing organisation, HR people meet hundreds of people from outside the company in the recruitment process alone, and interact by letter or e-mail with thousands. What a fantastic opportunity to establish the identity of the organisation in the market!

> ‹ We must constantly maintain
> contact with and strive to follow
> those recognised as best in
> class ›

Finally, I will highlight the area of benchmarking. We all have much to learn from the best in class. Andrew provides some excellent examples of benchmarking in his chapters. We must constantly maintain contact with and strive to follow those recognised as best in class. I don't just mean the HR gurus or the very good HR companies; this goes deeper than that. We need to participate in any exercise that seeks to develop the brand of our business in order to focus our activities on the consistency of internal and external brand.

The business partner in action

Every HR professional with ambition and an awareness of the strategic future of their organisation is seeking to be seen as a business partner. Their reasons may be based in the furtherance of their individual career, or it may be founded in a deep understanding of the future of the organisation and how this will be achieved.

The previous section on getting HR credible goes a long way to describing the role of HR today and to indicating the nature of business partnership. There is one more element of the role I wish to highlight. This is the aspect of HR that goes furthest towards the status of business partner. It is working with the head of the business function for which we have responsibility. In my case it has been the MD for the last few years, in a number of companies. Previously it has been a functional head, and I am especially proud of the working relationship I developed with the head of an IT division in the early 1990s.

This relationship was forged at a difficult time for the business. The company was in a significant period of downsizing, and the IT function was perceived as large and internally focused. Alongside the head of IT, we were able to simultaneously implement the necessary headcount reductions and a radical new, service-driven organisation. Even today, the project-managed organisation with clear interplay between the functional, people and project axes of the organisation would be considered fairly modern in many companies. At the time it was innovative and in the circumstances it was improbable. Some great people achieved rapid career progression as a result of the changes we made together, the function was recognised as making huge strides in support of the company and the head of IT and I became good friends.

My point is that the partnership between functional head and HR manager was key to the progress we made. So, how do we establish such a relationship with our central customer?

The answer is based on the premise that, while the MD (or relevant function or divisional head) needs to have his or her own eyes and ears throughout the business, the HR function is perfectly placed to give a second and impartial opinion. Such a second opinion might not be wholly supportive or well received – it is sometimes referred to as being the conscience of the organisation, but it must go further than that.

The first step is to have a valid opinion, which requires you to know what is going on. Here personal and professional integrity is paramount, as it requires people to trust you. If no one ever tells you anything truthful, how can you expect to be considered to have a valid input?

The formal part of this element of business partnering is found in succession planning, the development of feedback loops from internal communication, employee surveys and the formulation of input to the performance appraisal of the first line managers. These are key activities for HR people, but informal channels are equally important and need the same level of attention. The business partner HR function is seen by everyone in the company as relevant and capable of catalysing or facilitating change. Making the function relevant is probably the crux of the journey to business partner status, and there are many ways of achieving this – but essentially through facilitation, challenge and representation.

However, even if everyone in the company were able to tell us everything about the experience of employees, capability of managers and frustrations of organisation in the business, we only become business partners if we demonstrate credible insight into business and industry, and interpret and analyse the data accordingly. This comes from solid business acumen, analytical ability and judgement – all things HR people need to get at all costs if they really want to be business partners.

And finally, we all have to work hard to establish the right personal rapport and relationship with the head of the division or company we work with. I have good and bad experiences of this and have learned from each one. I refuse to mention names, but ultimately the role of HR is to ensure that this person is allowed to follow their nose only some of the time.

Summary

In describing the role of HR today, my focus has been on three areas:

❖ I have been privileged enough to have seen a number of excellent HR people in action in a relatively short period of time, and there are lessons to be derived from what they did.

❖ The role of HR is nothing without credibility and the majority of the chapter has concentrated on getting credible.

❖ The aim of the HR profession has been to achieve the nirvana of business partner status; much of that is about getting credible, but there are some close personal relationships to be achieved, managed and nurtured along the way if that is really to be achieved.

The role of HR today, at least in my opinion, is set out here:

❖ *Delivering the support service* – the administration, detail and welfare aspects of the HR role are often underplayed by those seeking to be recognised as business partners. This is inappropriate; these are the foundations of the role, without which we lose credibility and respect.

❖ *Delivering on promises* – the HR role cannot be punctuated by shrugging shoulders when things don't quite turn out the way we wanted, and if the obvious methods don't work we just have to keep looking for new ways to deliver.

❖ *Leadership on key HR matters* – too often we fail to grasp the key HR issues of the day and fail the company by allowing them to be dealt with piecemeal and without synergy and integration. Above all else, we must be able to take the lead on home-territory matters.

❖ *Being at the heart of culture and change* – achieving the appropriate culture and managing successful change simply must have HR involvement; it is inevitably the people and the communication issues that make the difference between right culture and wrong culture, and successful change programme and unsuccessful change programme.

❖ *Demonstrating a clear understanding of the business* – I argue that this is moving beyond simply being a tool for the job and into part of the job itself.

❧ *Simultaneously supporting and challenging the line* – the role of HR is not simply to deliver short-term internal customer delight; we must challenge effectively and stimulate change, even where this is not immediately popular.

❧ *Resolving the gap issues* – the HR role can no longer sit inside the boundaries of HR; there are key issues to be resolved that require leadership from HR even where this is off the beaten track for HR. We shouldn't empire-build, but nor should we let things ride that affect the integrity of the organisation and the motivation of the people.

❧ *Getting out of the office* – HR is not just an internal support role; if we're really going to demonstrate an understanding of the business and a contribution to taking the organisation forward, then we must understand the external context in relation to the employment market, the regulatory and social framework, and the competition. We must accept our role as ambassadors for the business with enthusiasm and vigour.

❧ *Becoming a true business partner* – no one will simply give HR the business partner badge. A business partner is seen by the rest of the management team as relevant and by the CEO or function head as crucial. Any less than this and we haven't made it.

References

1   BAHRAMI H. *and* EVANS S. (1997) 'Human resource leadership in knowledge-based entities: shaping the context of work'. *Human Resource Management*. Vol. 36, No. 1. Spring. p27.

2   BROCKBANK W. (1997) 'HR's future on the way to a presence'. *Human Resource Management*. Vol. 36, No. 1. Spring. p66.

Chapter 4

Leading change

Andrew Newall

Is culture important?

I can remember the drive to work that cold November morning.
It was my first official day at Allied Distillers Limited (ADL). It
rained the whole journey and, as a consequence, I took an hour
and a half – not the best start. Driving into Dumbarton I saw in
front of me the tall, red-brick building – a landmark in the town.
It looked every bit its 60 years. My immediate thought driving
up the potholed road was: had I made the right decision?

The place looked and felt old-fashioned. As I drove into the car
park I noticed that the gardens were manicured. The flagpoles
were draped with the colours of the foreign nationals visiting the
company. Visitors to the company were almost a daily occurrence.
The scene was symbolic of a company rich in tradition and full of
pride in its achievements and heritage. The receptionists were
friendly and effective. You can tell when a company is effective –
it meets you as you come through the door.

The office I was given was typical of the others in the building.
High, oak-panelled walls, deep-pile carpet, heavy wooden doors
and stained-glass windows. It felt more like a prison than a place
of inspiration. There was absolute silence, no buzz in the office
block. I would occasionally bump into a colleague in the corridor
and wonder if he too was lost. The best part was having my coffee
brought to me on a silver platter with a scone at 10.30am each
day. As I was addicted to coffee, being restricted to one cup in the
morning and tea in the afternoon because 'that's what we serve'
had me suffering from withdrawal symptoms.

The above examples of the culture are trivial, but they are the tip
of the iceberg. As you could probably tell, the business had a

somewhat confused culture. There was no doubt that ADL was successful. It had never failed to make a substantial profit, but its culture could be described, at best, as quaint and paternalistic and, perhaps more accurately, as far too traditional.

Every company has its own unique culture – and it gets into everything. It is essential to understand this, particularly if you are in the job of introducing change. How can you hope to introduce anything lasting unless you understand the culture you are dealing with? Its *depth* will also prove crucial in whether you will be able to get to grips with the real issues in the company.

‹ It is the leadership of a company that sets the tone ›

I do not intend to embark on some abstract analysis of the nature of culture and whether it really exists at all. For practical purposes, I believe that culture is a manifestation of behaviours and values within a business, and that has always been enough for me to do something about it. The behaviours that managers in particular exhibit come almost directly from the senior executives in any company. It is the leadership of a company that sets the tone – a tone that can become ingrained in almost everything HR is asked to address. Think about how behaviours affect the level of responsibility managers and ordinary individuals have within the company – how behaviours are shaped by the reward and recognition processes, the communication process and how individuals are measured.

It is possible to assess the type of culture that exists within a company. ADL in 1995 was somewhere between traditional and participative but experimenting with increased involvement in decision-making. From 1996 to 2000 we carried out a number of audits to establish in more meaningful detail the type of culture ADL exhibited, although we already knew that the culture at each location – as evidenced by the behaviours and attitudes of the people – was different.

The Strathclyde distillery was one of the best examples of this. Employees at this plant felt the strongest sense of identity.

Strathclyde is located 20 miles from Dumbarton and, until 1992, formed part of the Whitbread Group. Its strong sense of loyalty to the past can be directly traced back to the decision by ADL to harmonise terms and conditions. We reduced their earnings in line with those of employees based in Dumbarton. The people of Strathclyde never forgot our handling of the change process and regularly referred back to the 'good old days', often objecting to 'the Dumbarton way of doing things'.

Measuring culture

In 1998 and 1999 we commissioned a consultancy organisation to help assess the culture at our three main units in Dumbarton. These were Glasgow Road, the head office; Kilmalid, the larger of the two bottling halls; and Newtown bottling, which specialised in the low-volume, high-margin products. Collectively these three sites employed 1,143 employees in 1999.

The consultants provided a model for assessing culture based on a matrix of 15 key indicators. Analysis would determine where a particular culture was situated on a scale ranging from 'traditional' to 'mature self-directed'.

Traditional cultures tended to have organisational styles built upon command and control structures where positional power was the main driver. Such a culture can be characterised by:

- senior executives rarely seen, making decisions on high
- management determining targets, usually on the basis of what is achievable in comparison with the previous year's performance
- teams rarely seeing the results
- development limited to on-the-job training or courses organised by the personnel department
- employees not encouraged or expected to become involved in decision-making, supported by an attitude of *park your brain at the door*
- reward and recognition financial in nature and determined by the manager

top-down communication, normally by noticeboard and the occasional team briefing

 change programmes limited to big bang initiatives.

Mature, self-directed organisations were at the other end of the spectrum. Organisational structures and style were built around business teams based upon products, processes and customers. They were characterised by:

 senior managers inspiring employees to innovate to improve the business

 employees close to the customer expected to articulate and understand their needs, and to adapt to reflect any changes

 teams setting targets, with measurement geared to seeking improvements in results based on learning

 development needs determined and addressed by the individual

 recognition and reward determined by the team and acknowledged throughout the business

 initiatives constant and integrated with other business-wide schemes

 fact-based communication with job-holders sharing knowledge regularly

 feedback institutionalised, with individuals seeking wide-ranging sources to improve themselves.

Having established where we were on this spectrum we compared ourselves with best in class organisations. This determined the gap between our culture and the top-performing companies. We then set ourselves targets for moving each cultural indicator towards the mature self-directed style (although not all of them shifted to the same extent).

By taking such action you begin to shape the company you want. By measuring yourself against the best you start to drive performance.

Results of cultural analysis

As expected, the results on each site were quite different. Newtown was the most traditional site, but the profile of its culture showed the greatest consensus and alignment. Kilmalid had the least clarity. Inconsistency in the perceived roles of the middle managers led to individuals and subgroups operating independently. Management had become more strategic, but the organisational structures to support decision-making and accountability were not robust enough to achieve the desired business results at team level.

There is no doubt that the culture changed during the five years I am describing. We became more performance-oriented, with individual employees having a greater say in the destiny of the company, and we would often invite them to contribute to the content and design of our strategy.

Culture, as I have said above, matters – it shapes how you do business and how people feel about the company, but it is important to realise that it is organic. It's something that grows wild or something that can be shaped like the manicured gardens that I saw as I drove through the gates of ADL for the very first time. All it takes is some effort and an understanding of what you are doing.

Introducing change – create a crisis

Cultural change does not simply happen. Some form of intervention needs to take place in the first instance. Even evolution, the slowest form of change, happens as a consequence of adjustment to a changing environment. Someone needs to intervene. That person need not be a human resource specialist. HR specialists, however, need to master the techniques of change management.

ADL was not in a state of crisis. It was a successful business making a substantial contribution to the profitability of Allied Domecq. Not for the first time when I explained why we need to challenge the status quo and consider new ways of working, I got the stock reply: 'We make a very good profit. How much money do you want to make?' The response almost implied that we, the company, were becoming greedy.

There is always a reason for change. You simply have to raise your eyes and look for it. Allied Domecq, the parent company, knew this in 1994 – and so, to be fair, did the board of ADL. Not all of the senior management team accepted this, though, and the wider population rejected the need.

In my first few weeks, as I was shown around the production facilities and I asked the usual questions, I soon realised that measuring performance was not seen to be important. Delivery to the customer was important, but with a very full supply chain, stuffed with product, 'on-time and in-full delivery performance' was not that critical. Profit was created at the very top of the organisation, with the rest of the organisation focusing on quality and service. Cost was less of an issue. Many of the managers I spoke to in the early months had no idea of the size of their budgets, nor how much they were spending against budget. This led to the standard solution to any problem being to buy it out. With good margins, service to the consumer was paramount.

Much of the recognition of the need to change was driven by an expectation from the City following the successful change programmes taking place by the competition.

In 1995 City institutions owned 77 per cent of Allied Domecq. As in most businesses, performance and perception drove share price. The general perception was that the main board was a team (rather than a one-man band) that knew the business and had good strategic vision. One of the analysts at the time claimed that the board did the right things but they tended to take longer than our competitors to do them and, as a consequence, didn't come across as being particularly effective.

Like other stakeholders, the City needs confidence. Share price was driven down when the City was hit with a series of surprises in 1994 and 1995. The positive news at the time, though, was that, against the sector, Allied Domecq was 'very stable'. It is not the most motivating of comments to be told you are no worse than the rest and excel at maintaining the status quo. But the crisis for Allied Domecq came when the City began to show signs of losing patience. From this impatience the company embarked upon a radical improvement plan that would have HR at the very heart of it.

Change management is a skill

The need for change was recognised by Allied Distillers as early as 1994 and plans were in place to introduce teamworking and drive performance. The change programme was known as Project STAR – Skilled Teams Achieving Results. The objective was a flatter hierarchical structure with production personnel operating as teams. It addressed antiquated demarcation arrangements and ineffective working practices with reward systems and grading aligned with the new ways of working. All employees would be up-skilled and have their own personal development plan. The focus was on behavioural training, including team training and problem-solving. Despite considerable investment, the change programme fell at the first hurdle.

Analysis at the time concluded that there was no clear understanding of what the business was trying to achieve. The team leading the project had no experience of change management, hampered by a combination of the managers' mature ages, substantial length of service and lack of experience outside ADL. The proposed organisational structures at Kilmalid and Newtown were incompatible with empowered employees. There were too many managers and supervisors. The existing behavioural style at the warehouses and in the maturation department was especially disempowering.

An understanding of the complexity and fragility of the change process was confined to a handful of executives. Only a minority of managers regarded STAR as a platform for introducing entirely new methods of management and a continuous improvement culture. The break with the past was characterised by managers as uneven, haphazard and driven by a handful of senior figures. The general perception was that STAR was only about driving down costs, with the result that the key stakeholders, middle managers, supervisors, shop floor and trade unions failed to become engaged.

At the time, ADL's personnel department and unions were identified as the main institutional blockage to change. 'They're awkward, they give you brick walls. Together they constitute a single conservative bureaucracy. They have a vested interest in tying you up in knots. They both see the demise of the other as a danger to each other.' These were some of the comments made at the time.

Personnel were also the custodians of the agreements, principally the 1973 (GMB) and 1979 (AEEU) agreements, which itself tells you something about change. As custodians they were also very powerful. They were the only function that understood the content of the agreements and they were the function that interpreted the agreements. This intensified their power. It was not too surprising that under Project STAR they were completely excluded from the process.

When the project was finally wound up, a number of weaknesses were identified:

- ❖ no clear strategy, plan or rationale for the need to change
- ❖ no watershed event – a clear signal that change was coming
- ❖ no clear indication of the radicalness required
- ❖ no organisational analysis prior to launch and no involvement from stakeholders
- ❖ no involvement of personnel, despite being a people project
- ❖ unions openly opposed to the change programme
- ❖ no communications strategy and, therefore, no buy-in from stakeholders
- ❖ managers asked to take on the demands of the project as part of their normal job without much support, with the result that during the busy period the project was abandoned
- ❖ no clear definition of what 'teamwork' meant, resulting in different interpretations that fuelled suspicion
- ❖ no intermediate milestones or clear forms of measurement
- ❖ seen as simply a fad that had no corporate clout behind it
- ❖ widely regarded as a one-off project, rather than as a first step towards a new way of managing.

The key lesson from Project STAR was the need to recognise that change management requires some specific skills, clearly thought through in advance with contingency plans in place to deal with the unexpected.

Ingredients of change management

The failure of Project STAR was the catalyst for a radical shift from a personnel set-up to the introduction of a human resources function. The remit of this new team was quite unequivocal: to introduce change. They brought the following elements into the change programme:

- ❖ a communication strategy that explained the need for change, with implementation designed like a marketing campaign
- ❖ an analysis of the power of the major stakeholders, assessing the power bases of each (while recognising that power could be either a positive or negative factor in the attainment of our objectives)
- ❖ an understanding of the barriers to change and workable contingency plans to address them
- ❖ a review of the resources needed, including finance, time, external support and people
- ❖ details of how change was to be bedded in the business strategy, with recognisable business benefits
- ❖ clear milestones marking progress and manoeuvrable targets.

We also adopted the following basic philosophical attitudes:

- ❖ a desire to build trust at all levels, which has to be earned and is demonstrated through behaviours
- ❖ a philosophy of congruence, which positively promotes partnership, based on a genuine belief that all parties should gain
- ❖ a determination to maximise involvement in both the design and implementation of the change process
- ❖ a naïve hunger for learning and experimentation; this required a comprehensive review of what the competition was up to and identification of who the 'best in class' organisations were; it also required an open mind and willingness to learn from anyone.

Leading change is not easy, particularly if it is cultural change you are trying to introduce. Change agents need to master their trade. It is not something you simply do. You need to know what to do and how to do it (although environmental factors can always undermine your efforts). Look at it this way: you don't simply pick up a guitar and start playing. You need to learn how to play.

Change management is no different. Project STAR is a good example of the risks of embarking on a change programme without mastering the techniques.

Developing communication professionalism

Good communication is critical to achieving success in almost anything, and it was certainly vital to our plans to introduce major change and turn ADL around. Prior to 1996 most of the communication at ADL focused on 'good news stories' about growth in sales – often in markets in which we had very little share! No wonder the picture looked good. There was very little about how the company was performing and nothing about what the competition was up to. In 1995 we had one person in communication, constantly frustrated by the lack of understanding of its power. By 2000 we had a communication department of four people, producing our own newspaper, *Straight Talk,* and a TV centre that we called our creation station. The focus had grown from only internal communications to corporate affairs. We set out to describe to politicians and the business community what ADL was about and how it was making a contribution to the Scottish economy.

The MD, Ian Gourlay, was a strong believer in the power of communication, but for him effectiveness with a top-down approach was not enough. I could not agree more. For him upward communication and horizontal sharing of information were more important. In order to unlock the potential, our people needed to understand why we had to change and we needed to understand their expectations and concerns. Everything was about to change: the relationship we had with our suppliers and customers, organisational structures, terms and conditions of employment, the tasks that people performed, the numbers of people in the business and how we competed. The biggest challenge would be to change the behaviours. This could never be pain-free, but excellence in communication could at least ensure it would be understood and accepted (although I don't mean 'accepted' without challenge!).

Change needs to start from within. If people are going to accept it, they need to know why and how it affects them. They are even more likely to accept it if they can shape how it affects them. Change is always very personal.

Top-down and bottom-up communication

Advances in communication technology should have improved the effectiveness of information-sharing in organisations. With e-mail, intranet and video and audio conferencing it should be possible to ensure that the message gets across. However, technology is never the key issue; people are. I noticed a marked reduction in my e-mails and faster communication when we moved into open-plan office accommodation. People could see one another and would wander up for a chat rather than send an e-mail.

‹ Good communication is not just about influence; it also requires imagination and creativity ›

If communication is to be effective it needs to be planned as meticulously as a marketing campaign. We had at least 14 channels of communication at ADL. It is also worth stressing that good communication is not just about influence; it also requires imagination and creativity. This is because each channel will have a limited life and will fade in effectiveness unless reinvented or rejuvenated. During major change initiatives each was used to reinforce the key message we wanted to put across and obtain immediate feedback on what people thought. This enabled us to adapt our plans to make the change more acceptable without compromising on our ultimate objectives. More often than not we also captured some excellent ideas.

It is worth commenting on some of the channels used, remembering that feedback is always an integral part of the process.

Straight Talk

This is our in-house company newspaper, introduced in 1996 and designed to look, read and feel as though it was the *Daily Record.*

We engaged part-time professional reporters to write articles and sought the advice of a local newspaper on content and layout.

The objective of the paper was to tell the good news and the bad. In addition, it was a vehicle to capture what ordinary people thought about everything from corporate strategy to pricing changes in the restaurant. Stories and opinions were printed unedited and all questions were answered in print, regardless of how personally difficult for the manager targeted.

Breakout sessions

We launched these to let employees understand that directors were human too. More important, we wanted the directors to reach out to ordinary people. Breakout sessions were designed to take place, ideally in an informal setting, at the employees' place of work. There was no formal agenda: directors were there to answer questions. To support them, we trained each in media studies and how to handle awkward questions.

Annual workshops

These evolved from management-only conferences in 1996 to events anyone could attend. By 2000 we would address up to 600 people over a five-day period. The content changed from senior management presentations, with little audience participation, to employees taking centre stage and celebrating their achievements with their colleagues.

Roadshows

At the start of our financial year, the MD would visit each of our 20 sites and explain the business environment. He would speak to all employees and give them the opportunity to ask questions. The purpose was to describe our vision and key targets and ensure there was alignment and buy-in for what we needed to achieve. An additional benefit was to reinforce the human side of the top team. It's easier for people to buy in to something if you can put a face to the policy.

Cascade briefings

We classify information into different categories. Items marked red were cascaded immediately from the top of the organisation to all employees. Other types of message could be managed locally. The purpose was to ensure that our employees were aware of what was happening before it hit the external press and could, therefore, affect morale.

Towards 2000

This was a quarterly update on business performance attended by key stakeholders, management, employees and shop stewards. Given that much of the content was commercially sensitive, it was also a demonstration of the trust we had in our employees and the trade unions. Demonstrating trust helped us gain trust.

Presidential address

The chairman speaks to all employees at the same time.

Special briefings

These are sessions where external speakers would discuss particular topics with employees. Speakers included government ministers, MPs, senior trade union officials, members of the media, university professors and customers.

Letters to the home address

These can be effective to begin with, if used sparingly, although we were told people would often rather read the cereal box!

Team briefings

HR seemed to be constantly reminding the business of the importance of team briefings and training managers on how to carry them out. They were designed to address local issues but usually carried a corporate message.

Finally, we also spent a lot of energy communicating with the local community, other business leaders and MPs. Activities included running business conferences on 'best in class' in conjunction with the CBI and visiting MPs at the Scottish Parliament to reinforce our message that ADL could play a leadership role in the Scottish business community.

Leading full-frontal change

Managing change requires the abilities to paint a vision of what life will look like tomorrow and to ensure the business gets there. For ADL major change occurred both incrementally and as big bang initiatives. In both cases, however, it was planned meticulously and the formula was identical. HR can either lead change or play a major role partnering the major protagonists. The critical factors are the competency, confidence and courage of the HR professionals.

In this section I want to describe two big bang changes that took place in ADL from 1996 to 2000. Both are examples of where the status of the HR team rose to that of business leaders through vision and change mastery. They also contain techniques that can be adapted to many other circumstances.

Example 1: the Change Agenda – becoming a business partner

This initiative was planned, designed, executed and, more importantly, led by the human resources team. We could not have achieved it, however, without the vision and challenge of senior managers, employees and trade unions. It also changed the perception the business had of HR. We were no longer a support function but a contributor to business strategy and bottom-line profit. We now had a seat at the table and senior managers listened to our recommendations on matters not restricted to HR. We were no longer a support function but a function that led.

In business, change is often perceived as a mechanism for creating a differential advantage. That's not how it was for ADL. We just wanted to catch up with the rest. In 1996 our two main competitors realised that customers' tastes were moving away from brown spirits. They claimed that as an industry we had lost a generation. In some markets Scotch was perceived as an old man's drink. The sector had become sleepy and complacent. One of the competitors woke up to this and launched a change programme built on partnership with its employees but aimed at driving up both efficiency and effectiveness. Other competitors were shocked into action and were off the blocks and well down the track before we realised we were in a race. We soon learned that we needed better intelligence on what the competition are up to.

Planned change?

The changes at ADL, both the full-frontal initiatives and the pincer movement (which I will cover in the next section), were planned in advance and supported by well-executed communication campaigns. I did not have the patience for emergent change and the business could not wait that long.

In theory, planned change originates with a decision by the business deliberately to improve its functioning, followed by management informing everyone of the desired change and articulating a shared vision to gain commitment to the future state. Let's get real for a minute. This was not how it happened in ADL. We had no idea what we wanted to create. All we knew was that we did not like what we had and our vision was no more than to make tomorrow better.

Dealing with resistance

HR professionals should not become disheartened or frustrated when they encounter resistance. You are dealing with a perfectly natural human reaction. We need to get below the fear factor and deal with the underlying assumptions. Sometimes you need to give people time for it to sink in, which also requires you to have fine-tuned influencing skills, particularly with management colleagues who may be even less patient than you.

Achieving buy-in

When you lead change you need to give as much time to all the stakeholders. We spent three months selling the Change Agenda upwards. We were asking for £8 million to make the change happen, so our arguments had to be robust. As part of the selling process we analysed:

- ❖ the resource we needed
- ❖ the benefit on a return-on-investment basis
- ❖ the power each stakeholder had (down to the level of key pro-

tagonists), how we believed each would react and how we would overcome resistance

◆ how we would implement each element of the change process and the resource we would need to make it happen

◆ how we would communicate the changes both internally and externally and what channels we would use

◆ how our proposals linked back to the business strategy.

Build a competent team around you

We pulled together a diverse group of senior managers and high-potential middle managers to help design the change. It was important that line management felt part of the design process. In this way we gained their buy-in as we worked up the plan.

Build in sufficient time for the task

How many times during a negotiation are you frustrated by the loss of momentum and grounded by the need to break off discussions to accommodate diary constraints? In this instance, we locked ourselves in a hotel for three weeks in November 1996 and worked at each issue until it was resolved. We wanted to control the communication process and it was easier to have all the stewards with us off-site. They soon became a source of inspiration.

Build trust

The HR professional needs to get below the public face of the individuals they are dealing with and reach the person underneath. Week one of the negotiation was the typical growling and snarling at one another. By the end of that week both sides began to realise we were only human. This was achieved through the close proximity and intensity of the environment we were in. The union soon realised that we did not have all the answers – and at one stage questioned whether we had any! We had gone to the table knowing what we wanted to change and what we were prepared to pay for it but not what we would put in its place. The unions forced us to work out the detail, claiming they could not ballot 'their members' on the unknown. This forced the management team to raise their game and trust the union. By demonstrating trust we gained trust.

Be creative

We had begun with six members in the management team facing 32 shop stewards and three full-time officials. The document we presented was seven pages long and full of 'motherhood statements'. By the end of week two we had more management involved in the negotiations than union and the paper grew into a detailed 47-page booklet. Small groups allocated to particular tasks produced recommendations on issues including:

- ✤ new harmonised terms and conditions
- ✤ new grading structures and payment arrangements that ended all local allowances
- ✤ new up-skilling and multi-skilling programmes, which involved the group visiting the competition and local colleges
- ✤ new systems of working, increasing flexibility and ending demarcation
- ✤ guarantees of employment to 2000 (which has now been extended to 2002)
- ✤ new family-friendly policies – before they became fashionable.

Maximise involvement

To ensure that all managers felt involved we held weekly briefing sessions back at the plant. We informed them of progress and sought their advice on what we should do next. If a change is to be successful, management must demonstrate their commitment and feel that they have contributed in some way.

Use creative communication

In the third week we concentrated on selling what we had designed, and here the communication machine kicked in. Both management and union stood on the same platform and sold the content and benefits of the Change Agenda at all 15 sites it affected. Where we thought we would not have enough votes we went back and tried to address concerns in the final draft of the booklet. We reproduced it in plain English and sent copies to employees' home addresses. We even wrote to their partners – anyone we felt could influence opinion. Through the trade unions we invited in the local MP and he too wrote to employees on parliamentary headed paper urging people to support the deal.

Finally, we also brought in reporters from the local newspapers and told them how this was a good news story for Dumbarton, and they printed a story that recommended our employees accept the deal. The ballot gave a 75 per cent return in favour.

Introduce agreed change immediately

❛When you reach agreement on a change, do not hesitate in introducing it❜

Following the Christmas break we immediately introduced all the changes. When you reach agreement on a change, do not hesitate in introducing it. Close down the option to go backwards by ensuring there is no option but to go forward.

The Change Agenda was without question a well-executed change programme, although it took a further 18 months for the company and our people to realise the true benefits. It was strategically linked to the objectives of the business and raised the profile of the HR team in Scotland to the status of business partners. We demonstrated that we had understood the bigger picture and had the ability to make things happen. Now management would not consider change without the input from HR. We were managers who happened to specialise in human resources.

Example 2: building on success – painting the vision

This project concerned the building of a new office complex and factory and the consolidation of activities on the Kilmalid site. The board had taken the strategic decision to give ADL an advantage over all other major spirit producers in Scotland. We would be the only major player with all activities in one location. Over 400 people were involved in this project. The role of HR, to a great extent, was to create the environment where people would willingly want to get involved through having the courage and ability to influence strategy.

On 21 January 1999, the directors of ADL relayed MD Ian Gourlay's message concerning our latest project, Building on

Success (BoS). Each director took a different plant and in front of every employee shared what we believed was good news for the people of ADL. We spent two months crafting the message. It was the first time employees had heard of our plan and, despite knowing it was good news, we were nervous about how it would be received. It was important that our people fully understood the true meaning of what we were saying.

In simple terms we had secured a £20 million investment from Allied Domecq to build a new factory and office complex and consolidate activities at Kilmaild. We would close the office complex at Glasgow Road and the Newtown bottling hall and operate with 150 fewer people. This was potentially a shock, given that since 1995 the number of people we employed had halved and here we were telling them there were more to go. We softened the blow by extending our guarantee of employment to 2002 and reaffirmed that there would be roles for everyone that wanted to stay in the business.

We told all employees that this was good news both for them and for the people of Dumbarton, and we promised that:

 we would involve all employees in the project who wanted to be involved; over time this amounted to over 400 people playing some role in the design and implementation of our new premises

 we would return Kilmaild to the state of the art unit it had been in the 1980s and that it would be the envy of the competition

 we would create something the competition did not have and could not replicate easily

 we would benchmark and incorporate the best ideas from the best organisations.

We kept all of these promises.

I made the presentation to the people of Kilmalid. The plant manager was with me and together we told the 'whole story'. At the end of the presentation, which included a video from the MD, we took questions and answers. There were not many. After a short silence the place broke into spontaneous applause. I have made lots of these presentations in my career but this was the first time management was applauded. Despite stressing that we were closing a factory and an office block and that 150 people would leave the business, people were applauding. I have to admit it was somewhat emotional.

This reaction stuck in my mind for a few days and I grappled with the question of why people were applauding. It took a while, but eventually it dawned on me. They were not applauding the news – they were applauding themselves. Had it not been for their magnificent turnaround in performance and change in attitude, the board of Allied Domecq would not have provided ADL with the money it needed. What the board had shown was confidence in ADL. The people of ADL proved they could deliver and were prepared to face any change and challenge with maturity. It should be stressed that ADL was competing for this investment; there was no guarantee we would receive it. This was one of the first tangible signs that the culture HR were trying to create was coming to fruition.

Recognise achievement, celebrate success

The seeds of recognition that ADL was a different company sprouted for me in June 1998 when we hosted the human resources leaders forum at ADL. Every quarter the HR leaders of Allied Domecq would meet to discuss strategy. They would visit different locations and take the opportunity to find out what was happening 'at the coal face'. ADL was well known by reputation. Only three years earlier the employees were threatening strike action.

The normal process was for each HR leader to make a presentation on key activities and list what we had achieved. I wanted to do something different and, along with the departmental manager for Kilmalid, planned something special: the people of ADL would speak for themselves. By now we had spent some £1.5 million on training and the benefits were flowing through. Every indicator was showing substantial improvement. We decided the people themselves should both present their achievements and demonstrate them on-site with staff acting as guides. HR and line management would take a back seat. People would tell it as they saw it.

Employees who had gone through basic literacy and numeric training only months earlier now stood in front of senior managers from all across the globe. They wrote the presentation themselves and told it straight from the heart. The pride in the faces of each operator as they described their role and the new skills they had learned was evident for everyone to see. HR did not need to say anything: the employees of ADL said it for us. At the end of the day we invited everyone – visitors to the company, the Board of ADL and all employees who had been involved in the day – to a barbecue on the banks of Loch Lomond. Over 60 people attended and there was no them and us. Following this visit, the achievements and reputation of ADL spread within the group and within the business community. This was positive PR designed and executed by HR.

In October of the same year we had the full board of Allied Domecq visit Kilmalid. It was the first time they had been there for a number of years. The June meeting turned out to be a dress rehearsal for what we ran in October. A month later the board approved our capital investment request and the Building on Success project was born (for further details, see Chapter 5).

Pincer movement change

‹ The minimum level of performance we are prepared to accept is the best of the competition ›

This statement, something I picked up from one of the lecturers I had at Warwick University, became a cliché at ADL. From 1996 to 2000 we launched a number of departmental reviews, each designed to raise the competency and performance levels of specific functions. This was not a big bang approach, but one where we targeted areas that we believed were underperforming.

Act as a facilitator

The role of HR in this situation is to facilitate change. It is not our role to find solutions but our responsibility to ensure that solutions are found. In ADL we have used this approach eight times and each occasion has brought reward both for the company and its employees. When faced with the evidence that shows you are way down the league table of performance, most people respond. The challenge for HR was not so much the 'change management' element in itself, but the demands of dealing with a large number of changes going on at the same time.

Operations review

This was effectively a stock-take of the management population and covered employees from director level through to first-line supervisors. Using assessment centres, psychometric testing and analysis of their track record, we evaluated this group. The exercise took almost eight months and, as a consequence of our findings, almost one-third of them left the business. The review took place before the Change Agenda and was the catalyst for things to come. Employees in the business got the message that we were serious about change.

Pincer movement reviews

Over five years we reviewed no fewer than eight different functions, from transport and operations to finance and logistics. It should go without saying that personnel was reviewed before any of the others, which led to the creation of the HR function. The total savings from these reviews were just under £8 million. More important, in each area departmental performance was substantially improved. In simple terms, we were identifying our weakest link and strengthening it and we told all those involved that was exactly what we were doing.

Our formula for pincer change – the transport review

The formula for each review was almost identical. The role of HR was to facilitate. It was not our responsibility to lead. A good example was the transport function. Management had gathered evidence that, despite providing a quality service, it was considerably more expensive than what we could have had from a third party.

Our first task was to share our beliefs with the employees in this function and inform them that we would be inviting in consultants to establish 'the facts'. Over the five years we used a variety of consultants. Their role was to investigate and, if correct, validate our suspicions. They would benchmark our performance against the competition and 'best in class' organisations. Having gathered the facts they would recommend corrective action to bridge the gap. In the case of the transport function the consultants confirmed that it was £500,000 more expensive than quality third parties. The only option to bridge this gap was to outsource the function.

Given the cultural change we had undertaken, I asked the MD how much he was prepared to accept to keep the function in-house. He settled on a sum of £350,000. I presented both options to all employees in the department. The choice was to outsource and save the full amount or find £350,000. After a lengthy debate they formed a task force and faced up to the challenge.

The role of HR was firstly to explain why current performance was no longer acceptable, even though it was argued that rates of pay had been negotiated by the management and the company and fell within the grading structure. This took some explaining. The service levels were good but they had 'priced themselves out of the market'. It took a number of weeks to get this message across. Once it had been accepted, HR's role was to keep the show on the road, offering support when needed and reminding employees of the urgency of finding solutions.

The transport team came up with 36 different suggestions and saved the company the sum it needed. Although these did not include reduced earnings, one idea was the introduction of annualised hours, something that would have been rejected if management had recommended it. They also proposed the disposal of half of the fleet and double day shifts (ie doubling up the use of vehicles rather than individual drivers each having their own). They also determined the most economical traffic routes in terms of fuel consumption. Now *that* was creative.

It took five months to conclude this matter. Leadership of the review rested with the departmental manager. Over time he built up considerable trust with his team, partly because they were all in it together, but also because he treated them with dignity and respect. Human resources did not lead this change but they were in the thick of it. We recommended consultation and full involvement, encouraging employees to take control of their own destiny rather than having someone make the decisions for them. To perform such a role requires influencing skills, patience, imagination and creativity.

Encourage involvement

You may argue that the transport staff had no choice but to get involved. I would disagree: people always have choices. We used this approach with all the functions that we reviewed, including a number that were core to the business (and so where outsourcing was not a viable option). In every case, they always became willingly engaged. I like to think that by giving people 'control', they will use it responsibly. I have not been proved wrong yet.

Summary

‹Culture affects everything an HR professional is asked to change›

If you are in the business of change you need to understand the organisational culture you are addressing and why it is important. Culture affects everything an HR professional is asked to change, and its depth will indicate to what extent you are likely to be successful in altering deep-rooted traditions and ways of doing things. Fortunately culture can be measured, so take time out to understand what you are dealing with.

Culture change does not simply happen: some form of intervention needs to take place. You can always find a need for change, but the rationale needs to go beyond the level of challenges that can always be expected. The HR professional is instrumental in establishing the need and ensuring that it is understood.

Hence communication is a critical ingredient in successful change management. Effective and imaginative communication will win you the hearts and minds of the people within your organisation. By ensuring that everyone has a say and testing understanding, you are laying solid foundations for the change programme. In order to unlock the potential, your people need to understand why change is needed and the company needs to understand the expectations of the stakeholders the change affects.

The management of change is a learned skill – and it's worth remembering that leading change, particularly cultural change, is never easy. By learning the essential ingredients you are more likely to succeed in your task of transforming outmoded systems into a culture in tune with the needs of the business.

Change can occur in a number of ways. It can be planned or evolutionary, big bang or incremental. All present crucial opportunities for the human resources function, which must master the ability to manage change. This requires it both to help paint the vision of the future and to ensure that the business gets there. The key factors are technical and business competency, confidence and courage. HR professionals can – and must – develop each of these.

Chapter 5

The organisation
that learns

Andrew Newall

Why learning is so important – understanding 'best in class'

Stop and think for a minute what you admire most in people or organisations that are somehow special. They are likely to have built and adapted the ideas of others, to take risks and show a desire to experiment. They are, in other words, innovative. The type of innovation that leads to breakthrough and the creation of something new depends crucially on *learning*. This will occur only in an environment where people feel safe.

Who better to seek out organisational learning and encourage the application of ideas than HR professionals? They are instrumental in shaping the environment within the company. Few functions are as well networked and willing to discuss experimentation and learning; it seems to be in our blood. HR people must lead by example and encourage others to become inquisitive in order to unlock talents and potential. They can and must show leadership in spurring the business on to learn in many different ways.

Motivation and environment are important. Motivated people with nothing to fear do not need to be encouraged; they will normally seek out learning opportunities. They will not take risks, however, if there is much to lose and little to gain. At ADL, we set ourselves the objective of becoming best in class and we had to learn what that meant. This chapter captures the lessons we discovered on the way.

Organisations that fail to learn will go out of business

One of the things I find most frustrating about myself, and I've also noticed in many organisations, is how quickly we forget. Unless learning leads to change in behaviour, knowledge and skills we may have worked hard to acquire will be lost. HR professionals must encourage the adoption of systems and processes that reinforce behavioural change and the application of new skills.

We did not have a history of training or developing people at Allied Distillers. The personnel function had in the past organised courses for those who wanted or needed, for example, coaching on 'presentation skills' or teaching the latest computer software. We did not have a learning culture where people would take that first step without fear of failure. There were some people in ADL who thought they knew it all and did not need to learn anything. There was also the odd one or two who had no intention of learning. Fortunately, such people were in the minority and were eventually carried along with the tide of enthusiasm for learning. What is sometimes necessary, and often falls to the HR function in particular, is to take time to explain to people what they don't know. This is clearly a very sensitive task.

Organisations, or rather the people who work within them, need to learn; we have no choice on this matter. The business world is moving too fast for us to stand still and depend on yesterday's knowledge. Consider how we all depend on e-mail now. To stand still is to go out of business.

Understanding best in class

As business evolves and the demands on individuals change, performance management and, in particular, regular job reviews become critical. Overlying this is the need for good, effective and frequent communication reiterating why yesterday's performance and knowledge are no longer good enough.

Raising the competency of your people is critical. This is what we discovered at ADL. We had set ourselves the objective of becoming 'best in class'. We wanted to be as good as the best, and not just in the drinks sector, so our first piece of learning lay in defining what this meant. For us, 'best in class' organisations were those that were publicly recognised and regularly turned in a superb financial performance; all stakeholders were proud to be associated with them. The more we studied the subject, the more we began to realise that such companies possessed a number of common attributes, best summed up in Dr James Maxmin's hierarchy of needs. Jim was my CEO at Laura Ashley, and his theory is described in greater detail in Chapter 2. For our present purposes we can just say all 'best in class' organisations demonstrate that they are:

- ◆ strategically led
- ◆ employee-driven
- ◆ market-oriented
- ◆ operationally excellent
- ◆ competitively focused.

I explore each of these aspects below, although it is worth mentioning that at ADL we addressed them all in parallel (rather than hierarchically, as implied in Chapter 2).

Strategically led

Strategically led organisations need a *shared vision*. Keep the vision simple. In the time I was at ADL, MD Ian Gourlay would articulate that our 'destination' was to become 'best in class'. This required many things from the people of ADL, the most fundamental of which was recognition that life in the company would never be the same again. The message was simple and easily remembered – and employees often used a football analogy to make it even clearer. Who could disagree with the sentiment that we wanted to be the Manchester United of our industry?

> **‹ It was crucial that ordinary people understood and bought into the vision ›**

Our strategy was built on four cornerstones – people, supply chain, customer service and finance – and went into considerable detail about what we needed to achieve. Yet it was crucial that ordinary people understood and bought into the vision. This required frequent and simple communication, with huge emphasis on two-way dialogue. Roadshows clearly spelt out what we needed to do and annual workshops were a vehicle for celebrating what we had learned and achieved.

Employee-driven – the role of HR

Each function had cumulative three-year targets based around 'people' (as opposed to human resources). At the highest level, our strategy for people could be split into a determination to:

- ◆ develop an environment where all employees were motivated towards self-development, maximising use of their skills and efficiency improvements
- ◆ develop a workforce skilled and flexible enough to meet changing customer demands
- ◆ build an open communication style to continuously encourage people to accept change and improvement in the way they work
- ◆ develop stronger links with all employees whilst recognising the positive role that trade unions can play
- ◆ pursue least people-cost in the manufacturing and supply chain.

We supported each of those general points with up to four layers of detail. To give an example, second-layer targets for the year 1996 included:

- ◆ Establish working relationship with employees and the trade unions.
- ◆ Create understanding of the need for change.
- ◆ Develop a professional communication team and communication strategy.
- ◆ Secure a two-year wage agreement.

The third layer split the objectives into three specific areas, reflecting how I structured the function, namely communications, HR operations and organisational development. Each layer was directly aligned to the business strategy. The fourth layer had targets for individuals in the HR function.

The evolution of the people strategy and the detail behind it, while facilitated by the human resources function, was the brainchild of a wide cross-section of employees, including union representatives. As the years went by, trust grew and we provided more commercially sensitive information, believing that this would improve understanding of the bigger picture and therefore decision-making. This reflected our philosophy of involvement and empowerment, ensured commitment to the strategy and helped create the environment that would transform the business.

Market-oriented – creating a desired environment

It was equally important to us that the improvements we were striving for proved lasting and meaningful. We knew by 1997 that we were good at driving 'the numbers', but it needed to be more than that. Hence we were just as focused on trying to create a culture that:

❖ reduced the layers of hierarchy and put increased emphasis on teams
❖ redefined all the management roles from director to first-line supervisor, stressing empowerment and involvement
❖ up-skilled the individual employees, by treating them as adults with focus on the customer
❖ built a company identity that would secure external recognition and encourage people to take pride in being part of a successful organisation
❖ put the emphasis on performance-oriented target-setting and measurement
❖ focused on learning, development and recognition
❖ got all the different departments and teams to take ownership of communication.

In each of the above areas we sought to learn from others. If other organisations had found a solution to a problem we were wrestling with, we did not hesitate in approaching them. All of those we spoke to were more than happy to share their learning (although some of the 'best in class' initiatives were not best for our business and were therefore rejected).

Operationally excellent – learning from consultants

In Chapter 4 I discussed a form of change we regarded as a *pincer movement*. This did not rely on the big bang approach, but it had as much effect in shaping attitudes and driving performance. If you are serious about being 'best in class', one of the areas you need to focus on is operational excellence. We carried out extensive reviews of eight separate functions. Each led to substantial improvements on all our key indicators. A consultancy firm led each review. It was they who validated our view of the current performance and offered recommendations to improve. Rather than simply implementing the consultants' suggestions, we kept them as fall-back ideas and asked our people to find their own solutions.

Each review was challenging for different reasons. I have previously described our involvement in the transport review, and Chapter 6 looks at the maturation review. In both instances HR facilitated the change. This required courage, innovation, patience and the ability to influence. It was not our task to come up with solutions, but our duty to ensure that solutions were found and progress made.

We would not have achieved as much as we did without the challenge from the external consultancy firms we engaged. These brought considerable learning and opened our eyes to alternatives. I have often heard managers dismiss consultants as people who feed back to you what you already know, but at ADL this was not our experience. We entered the relationship not so much as customer and supplier but more as student and teacher.

Operationally excellent – performance management

In addition to ensuring that your processes have been 'fine-tuned', it is equally important to develop a culture focused on performance. At its most simple the objective of HR is to:

❖ build commitment
❖ drive performance.

To support this objective we introduced a performance manage-

Figure 12
PERFORMANCE MANAGEMENT MATRIX

HIGH	EVIDENCE	requires development	meets requirements	role model for others
	exceptional	results and objectives achieved exceed expectations; teamwork and key role behaviours below expectations	results and objectives achieved exceed expectations; demonstrates effective teamwork/ behaviours	objectives, results, teamwork and key behaviours are exceptional; role model for others
What	**effective**	results and objectives achieved meet expectations; key behaviours and teamwork below expectations	results and objectives achieved meet expectations; delivers all key behaviours and teamwork	results and objectives achieved meet expectations; role model behaviours and teamwork an example for others
	less than effective	results and objectives achieved; key behaviours and teamwork fall below expectations.	results and objectives achieved fall below expectations; key behaviours are met	results and objectives achieved fall below expectations; role model behaviours an example for others

LOW ———————————————— How ————————→ HIGH

ment tool (see Figure 12), designed on a matrix basis, with the aim of driving performance. This forms the 'what' element of the matrix. The 'how' dimension looks at behavioural competencies. If we were serious about building the culture we wanted over the long term, how we achieved 'the numbers' was as important as the immediate results.

We now use this matrix right across the organisation. To ensure consistency and equity, assessment of all employees is made by a committee comprising all 21 senior managers. The whole idea was discovered in another organisation introduced into the company by the HR function. We have adapted the tool over time to incorporate learned improvements.

Competitively focused

We aimed to learn from anyone and everyone, and that included the competition. We were either given or acquired copies of their change programmes and we introduced what we believed were their best ideas. Consultancy firms and such universities as Strathclyde and Stirling also proved to be a huge source of knowledge for us. In addition, we invited MPs, senior government ministers, professors, media specialists and anyone else we thought might be of interest. As with many of the initiatives HR introduced, we started by actively encouraging people to attend and ended up having to limit the numbers.

We aimed to develop our staff all the way from people in the offices and factories right up to director level. We introduced the courses and programmes that most organisations rely on, supported by personal coaching and mentoring. Two initiatives we introduced are worth describing in more detail:

❖ the Building on Success project
❖ Workbase.

Benchmarking best in class – Building on Success (BoS)

This was the name given to the project to build our new factory and new office complex described in Chapter 4. It provided us with an opportunity to extend our initiative of creating a new culture and is another example of where HR had to show leadership.

It was not unusual for us to pull the cream of the talent from ADL and set up a high-profile project team under a director. The BoS project differed from most by incorporating into the terms of reference the requirement to maximise involvement. By the end of the project, which was completed on time and within budget, we had some form of input from over 400 people.

‹Culture is not some esoteric concept that you cannot get your hands around. Culture is real›

As the project developed and the initial sketches for the new office block came back from the architects, it was pretty obvious to me that they had in some way failed to capture what we were trying to achieve. Culture is not some esoteric concept that you cannot get your hands around. Culture is real. It is something that you can both see and feel and therefore something you can shape. One of the crucial ingredients is the environment you work in, and we had an ideal opportunity to design the environment needed to create a company that was something special.

In keeping with our habit of involvement, I pulled together a cross-section of volunteers and gave them a specific remit. We focused on designing the new office complex and a similar team was created for the new factory. We needed to understand what 'best in class' offices looked like, how organisations went about the design process and what sort of issues we should consider. Hence the benefits of a cross-functional team. I ended up with 14 people in the group, each from a different discipline and including a representative from each function. My objective was to ensure not only that I had someone with the technical skills needed but also that each of the key stakeholders was represented. The team comprised:

- *human resources staff* – responsible for reviewing how the move would affect terms and conditions, office hours, teamworking and so on
- *facilities management* – responsible for reviewing restaurant arrangements, opening hours, energy systems and costs, hot-desking, lighting, colour schemes, furniture, gardens, heating and ventilation
- *information technology* – responsible for reviewing IT requirements, telephone systems, and the possible benefits of document centres rather than printers and PCs on each desk
- *receptionists* – responsible for reviewing telephone arrangements, mail handling, the design and look of reception and the management of guests and visitors
- *engineers* – responsible for ensuring we maximised the latest benefits in air management systems, building shape, energy usage and savings
- *customer service and finance* – responsible for deciding which

functions best sit together, how we could move to a paperless environment, art work, water features and so on.

From my own viewpoint I wanted to create something special where people felt excited to come to work. This we achieved. I also wanted a building shape that stood out and was visible to the general public. In short I wanted to create a wow factor. That's one of the reasons I personally visited a number of well-known buildings.

We produced a term of reference for the project team, had it approved by the board and circulated it to the rest of the staff affected by the move for comment. The next step was to identify organisations that had built an award-winning new office complex in the last five years. This was not too difficult: trade magazines and word of mouth soon gave us the answers. Waterside, the British Airways headquarters just outside Heathrow, invariably came top whenever we asked someone what they would recommend. So we organised a minibus and went on tour. (I even drove the bus until they complained about my driving!) We went to the BT building in Birmingham, BA in London, Scottish Amicable in Stirling, and Standard Life and Scottish Courage in Edinburgh. We also revisited our own offices in Bristol, London and Madrid. In total we visited 23 locations across the UK and the Continent. At each location we learned something new. Some buildings taught us the way not to do it. Key learning points included the need to build in flexibility to cope with potential growth in the number of staff. 'HR on Tour', as it became known, lasted about five weeks. After each visit we wrote up our findings and listed the best ideas. This was not mainstream HR activity but crucially important in the context of the culture we were trying to create. It's an example, if you like, of where HR had to show leadership to ensure the business did not lose the opportunity we had.

Workbase – three Johns and a Robert – building commitment

By the time we had got our act together and began implementing the training programmes we had designed, it was late 1997 (a year after the Change Agenda had been signed). Each department had area training co-ordinators, something I picked up from

Llanwern Steelworks. Both the up-skilling and multi-skilling programmes had their own joint working party. It was their remit to determine the content of the programme and to source potential training providers. We awarded the multi-skilling to the AEEU College. One of our objectives was to cement our partnership relationship with the AEEU. In reality, this turned out to be a minor benefit in comparison with what they taught us. The major advantage was the huge professionalism and the latest thinking they brought to us, not only on a technical front but also from a health and safety point of view.

Each of the working parties was chaired by the union convenor. I sat on the up-skilling committee to ensure progress and a senior production manager sat on the other with the same remit. As you would expect, the first step was to carry out some form of skills analysis to establish the skills gap. We knew what we wanted to achieve. The detail was contained in the Change Agenda document, which everyone now had a copy of – so there were no surprises. The problem we faced was the level of mistrust of their team managers we found, both among the operators and the craftsmen. Yet who could be better at assessing what someone could do than their manager? This was a hurdle we could not get over.

The issue caused a great deal of difficulty for the senior management team. On the one hand, we urgently needed a 'stock take' of the skills that existed in the business, since this was the only way of identifying the talent and skill gaps. It was perfectly feasible for a third party to carry out this task. Yet it was more logical for the team managers to undertake this review. They were the obvious choice and, besides, we wanted to build teams where team managers were seen as leaders responsible for their people. The production staff made it clear that they did not trust the judgement of 'their leader' – not surprising, perhaps, given that the manager's assessment could affect their pay.

The GMB came to the rescue by recommending we introduce a charitable organisation called Workbase, which specialises in adult numeracy and literacy training. They would work alongside the team managers to identify skill levels. We had been considering Workbase for some specialist work needed for a small number of our people. We extended their remit to include a detailed skills audit. Given the independence of Workbase, our people accepted this.

The up-skilling and multi-skilling training was initially on a needs basis. The desire to attend the training was very limited to begin with. Very quickly, however, the benefits of the training began to spread and others requested that they be given the opportunity. It was soon evident that the sort of life skills taught were also of value outside work. Within weeks everyone wanted to attend. We were happy to support this. Workbase were the key to unlocking a hunger for learning. The major benefit we saw, however, was the rise in personal confidence and the beginning of securing commitment. Both are critical ingredients in any change programme.

Soon Workbase was providing presentation skills training to anyone who wanted it. We put this to good use. There is one good example that has almost become a legend at ADL. It concerned four ordinary people from Kilmalid, none of whom had ever given a formal presentation. They were John Boyd and his colleagues, two of whom were also called John, so they became known as 'Three Johns and a Robert'. They spoke on behalf of the people of Kilmalid and they described their recent experience. They presented to senior executives from across the globe and main board members of Allied Domecq. Their presentation was so well received they ended up presenting to external visitors, including politicians and senior trade union officials. In the words of John Boyd:

> It's made me feel a lot better. No longer treating you as a commodity. That's the way it used to be: you used to just come in and do your job and go home. Now you are an asset. They want to train you to the highest possible position. In the long term this can only be good, not only for the effectiveness on the line but for customer service as well. Now you've got a chance to go forward. I've been with the company for 25 years and they used to say you couldn't teach an old dog new tricks. I am one of these old dogs that has been taught new tricks.

John's words reflected the feelings of many people at ADL.

By December 1998 we had carried out 31,000 hours of up-skilling and multi-skilling training under the direction of HR. We were serious about reinvesting what we had saved and we could see the return both in hard performance and in the softer morale issues.

Global learning

‘True value resides in the heads of the people you employ’

One of the benefits of being part of a global organisation is the opportunity to learn from other human resource practitioners across the world. I have visited a number of countries and I brought back key learning points from every visit. Perhaps it's naivety on my part, but the more I travelled abroad the more I was surprised at how similar the issues – and the solutions – seemed to be. All the human resource specialists seemed to read the same books, use the same language and follow the same fashions. I have found examples of excellence in HR in areas I did not expect. Our sister operations in Mexico and Singapore made me realise that what I was doing in Scotland was probably not anything special after all. It teaches you not to believe your own PR. In Mexico I learned about knowledge management before I had even heard the term in Europe. The other thing that stuck in my mind as I walked around the bottling halls of Los Reyes in Mexico City was the fact that they used the same machinery to produce their products. Everywhere I go producers seem to be using either German or Italian equipment. This reinforced in me something I knew anyway. You get some advantage by buying the latest equipment, but the advantage only lasts as long as it takes for the competition to do the same. It's all on the open market. The only real and lasting difference was the skills, commitment and drive of the people who worked in each unit. It is, after all, people who plan the use of the equipment, people who use it and people who maintain it. This is where I saw the real difference, and that's why human resources is so important. True value resides in the heads of the people you employ, a point brought out by Jon Sparkes in Chapter 9. HR practitioners should never forget this.

On a visit to Fort Smith, Arkansas, two things stuck in my mind. I had gone there to look at their 'visual factory' programme, something they had learned from Pepsi. The true learning for me, however, was the huge enthusiasm I felt whenever I spoke to anyone at Fort Smith. This plant had gone through as much change as we had in Scotland. Despite this, you could almost touch the wave of positive energy. They had a huge drive to achieve and were proud of what they had achieved. This is what I set out to replicate in Scotland. This had been achieved as a consequence of the people initiatives the Fort Smith management had introduced. Like us, their HR team had a detailed people strategy. Here are some of the highlights I picked up on a second visit in 1998:

- extend competency selection to all employees
- achieve improved employee opinion survey scores
- implement gainsharing for all
- train first-line supervisors in involvement and communication
- enhance management training in interaction, problem-solving and project management skills
- develop an operator certification programme
- introduce a sixth visual factory 's' process (over and above the celebrated Japanese '5 S's' model Pepsi had used to improve their manufacturing systems).

I am sure you can see where I got some of my ideas.

Development for all

There was little point in focusing all our efforts at the shop floor level and ignoring the rest of the business. We aimed to invest in all our people. As HR director you will have personal responsibility for the development of your colleagues. Part of your role is to support the MD in ensuring that the board members are as effective as they must be.

Personal one-to-one coaching was introduced to support the development of the 'top team'. We used Dr Adrian Atkinson and his team from Human Factors International. Over time I saw Adrian work his magic and each of the directors grow. In addition, he and Clive Morton both provided mentoring support. Mentoring is something we apply across the business. I am personally mentoring four people at this time – one of them on the other side of the Atlantic and one on the Continent. We chose people to mentor or accepted volunteers who demonstrated that they had the bug for learning. In this way we used the mentoring process to support the cultural change we were embarking on. The best mentors were those who believe in and promote the values we live by. Technical training for the 'top team' was provided by the Institute of Directors.

Another development initiative the human resources team introduced was what we called the Change Leaders Programme. This was one of the most holistic programmes I have ever encountered. Mark Brown, my business transformation manager, designed it. Again key stakeholders were consulted and participated in the design. The programme was targeted at middle managers and employees from production and engineering who showed the ability to progress further in the business. Participation was based on need rather than a 'sheep dip' approach and required both the employee and his or her manager to contract to the learning. We wanted to ensure that each manager took ownership of the learning. All of them are also trained to be personal coaches.

Departmental managers were involved in both the design and delivery of the programme, which again helped to ensure buy-in. It was designed on a modular basis and lasted one year. It was delivered in partnership by senior managers from ADL, the Centre for Strategic Manufacturing (Strathclyde University), PSA – Training and Development, and Sheppard Moscow. We also ensured through the design of the programme that each organisation was delivering just one programme, so there were no overlaps of material or contradictions. To reinforce the learning, the participants operated in learning teams supported by personal coaches. Each learning team met on a regular basis. Up to 30 participants took part each year.

Senior managers delivered modules on human resource skills, managing absence, commercial awareness, introduction to the supply chain, customs and excise awareness, and financial awareness. Strathclyde University delivered modules on critical and strategic thinking, total process control, designing the process, removing waste, moving the constraints and managing process reliability. Sheppard Moscow provided the leadership and influencing skills training. Again the core of the programme was cultural change and driving business performance. PSA – Training and Development trained the group on time management and presentation skills as well as coaching the participants on managing their projects.

Each participant had a project to deliver. The logic behind this was to ensure that the learning was applied. The participant answered to a project champion, normally from the department it covered, who ensured that the participant had as much resource as needed to deliver the desired outcome. Each project had to show business benefit. All of them led to improvements in some way. As part of the learning process the participants were required regularly to present progress to the board and their colleagues.

You may ask why we designed such an elaborate programme. The answer is simple. I discussed in the last chapter the importance of culture and the action we took to assess what we had and how human resources could support the drive to create a 'best in class' organisation. As a direct consequence of this work I asked Mark Brown to come up with a programme that would meet the cultural attributes we wanted to create. He was asked to look at no more than six of the 15 cultural attributes and this is what he designed. That's why strategy is important. As a human resources director you need to have the bigger picture in your mind, in our case in a written document known as our *People Strategy*. Each strand of HR activity needs to knit together and reinforce your ultimate goal of creating something special.

Summary

Continuous learning is now a survival issue. Depending on yesterday's knowledge is a recipe for disaster. To compete at the highest level it is an imperative that organisations hone and release the talent that each business processes. HR must take the lead role in shaping the culture that encourages an environment where everyone wants to learn and improve. Raising the competency of your people is critical. We set about becoming a 'best in class' organisation and this was one of the first things we had to learn. We learned that such organisations are almost invariably:

◆ strategically led, with all employees able to articulate the vision with understanding

◆ competitively focused, driven by the need to compete at the highest levels and well aware of what the competition is up to

◆ market-oriented, close to both the customer and the consumer, which requires research into their changing needs and the agility to respond quickly

◆ employee-driven, with highly competent people united by the desire to learn, innovate and experiment

◆ operationally excellent, with finely tuned processes and clear performance measures.

Mastery in all will take you well down the path of achieving best in class status.

As HR professionals you need to develop an attitude to learning that makes it a way of life. This should apply to everyone in the organisation, top to bottom. We did not have the time to re-invent the wheel so we set about learning from anyone and any organisation that we encountered. By creating a culture where people are encouraged to learn and share and are aligned to the business strategy, you are far more likely to produce an organisation that others will find difficult to replicate. Learning is the key to differential advantage.

Chapter 6

Sustaining
partnership

Andrew Newall

What is partnership?

Many organisations now claim to have achieved some form of
partnership – most with the trade unions, some with suppliers,
but very few with their employees and even fewer with the local
community. It's seen as a mechanism for building competitive
advantage. Many claim it is the key to unlocking the potential
that lies deep within organisations. It certainly helps build commitment to the ultimate goals of the company.

Such partnerships always share some fundamental principles.
They are built on trust, personal integrity and mutual respect. If
any of these is missing from either party, they will fail. Effective
communication is, therefore, a must. All stakeholders have the
right to raise their agenda and state their case. Often it requires
one party to encourage another to get involved. Employees in particular need to be given the confidence and skills to do so. And,
as in every human relationship, if you do not respect the person
you are dealing with, you will have no chance of making partnership work. Be clear what you mean and be prepared to explain it
in terms that everyone understands.

ADL first considered partnership in 1995. The focus was on
building a working relationship with the trade unions. As stakeholders they could not be ignored and could potentially undermine any attempts we made to change the business. Yet
partnership was a risky option, given that we were not really sure
where we were heading and that the relationship with the unions
was nearing breakdown. Very few organisations had embarked on

this approach in 1995, so HR was in the front line and required to show real leadership.

While much of this chapter will focus on building partnership with the unions and employees, the same techniques can be applied much more widely. Since the early days we have taken positive action to build partnership with suppliers, local people and the business community.

Importance of trust

Partnership arrangements that succeed are built on trust between people. We were not in the business of beating the unions into submission. There were suggestions on the management side about marginalising those who failed to become engaged, but HR would not sanction this approach. As so often, it is crucial for us as HR practitioners to stand by our convictions.

Partnership requires both sides to be up front and to let people know both the good news and the bad news. It's about doing what you say and keeping your promises. It means that everyone has a voice, which can only be achieved by encouraging and max-imising involvement. You need the infrastructure to ensure the communication flows in both directions and to recognise that partnership requires more patience. In 1995 messages at ADL were conveyed to employees by the unions. We made it clear from 1996 that we would not prevent the unions communicating to 'their members' but that in future we would also talk directly to 'our employees'. The unions were very suspicious to begin with, but we always invited them to briefings. HR made it clear that direct communication was a fundamental principle we would not compromise on. The unions began to help us write the script, they have shared the same platform to help us deliver the message and, in more recent years, they have 'let us get on with it'.

As a consequence of the partnership approach people are actively encouraged to take ownership and get involved. This has led to a huge turnaround in attitude. What's more, when involvement evolves into influence, it's difficult to differentiate who is managing and who is following. By 1999 we had people from all parts of the company and representatives from the unions work together – with access to commercially sensitive information – on business strategy.

‹Partnership can make a bottom-line impact›

We did not really know we were building partnership in 1996 – we sort of stumbled along. Yet by forging stronger relationships with employees, by recognising they are stakeholders who would welcome the opportunity to shape the direction of the business, you are creating an organisation that others will find difficult to copy – and that's a differential advantage. Partnership can make a bottom-line impact.

Partnership for ADL has proved to be an evolutionary concept. We aimed to establish a better working relationship with the unions and this soon developed into making real contact with our employees. By 2000 we were attempting to build a relationship throughout the supply chain, with local people, the business community and the Scottish Parliament. We began to recognise that there were many more stakeholders and that they could have an impact on the company performance in many different ways.

Building partnership at ADL

Partnership and change management go hand in hand. (Why consider partnership if you are satisfied with the status quo?) ADL had to change and in 1996 we began explaining why. One option was to drive through the change with no more than the statutory consultation requirements. This was unlikely to succeed, given the strength of the trade unions and the general attitude of employees in ADL. Besides, it was not the natural style of many of the senior managers responsible for the change process. If you believe in people to begin with, partnership is much easier to achieve.

On 19 March 1996 the managing director stood on a platform in a cold warehouse in Dumbarton and spoke to over 1,000 people.

He explained the need for urgent change throughout the company and how this would have to be the responsibility of every single employee. HR planned the event and helped write the speech. A completely silent workforce received the seriousness and urgency in his words. The difficulty was getting employee buy-in on the need for change and achieving a unified approach on how this would be done.

Change had occurred at the management level through the restructuring of the senior and middle management population. Many people left the business and new blood was introduced. ADL board positions were created for the human resources and logistics functions. Waste management systems and single-sourcing of packaging materials helped reinforce a mood of change. A review of the shape of our business resulted in large savings through disposals of malt distilleries. Yet despite these major managerial initiatives the key to unlocking untapped potential and talent lay with the majority of our employees, who remained unconvinced of any need for change.

Employees claimed they were being asked to change for 'change's sake'. The way they had always done it was still the preferred way. The fear of what change would bring was uncomfortable for employees and their desire to maintain the status quo was para-mount. This attitude was reinforced by reference to two agree-ments, which limited flexibility, negotiated with the GMB in 1973 and the AEEU in 1979. Could you believe it – we were being constrained in 1996 by documents written in the 1970s?

We had achieved some success with the GMB and the MSF in 1995, but there was very little trust and a great deal of fear shown by the AEEU. They believed that they had everything to lose and nothing to gain. What was clear to us, though, was that building partnership with some but not all of the stakeholders was doomed to failure. When invited to meetings, the AEEU shop stewards would often stress that they had a 'listening brief' and could not participate. It's a bit like having your favourite aunt at a birthday party saying she was happy just to look on but not take part in the celebration. It sort of spoils the party.

Giving up was not an option. If you want to make tomorrow better, you have to work hard at it. We did the usual things like setting up a steering committee, a joint management/union body designed to deliver the changes that had been agreed in 1995. Looking back, they were pretty small items, but at that time it felt like an enormous hill to climb. We sourced a number of companies who could help us with teambuilding. If the steering committee was going to work it had to gel into a single unit with a common goal. We concluded that the GMB College in Manchester was our best option (and a demonstration that we recognised the professionalism of the GMB). The informal exchanges there helped challenge the perceived barriers between management and stewards.

We also did some unusual things. With the support of the full-time officers we made arrangements with the local colleges to educate the shop stewards. We taught them how to present a case and negotiate. This proved to be significant. Other small signals like taking time out to visit the unions' offices, rather than always expecting the full-time officers to visit us, showed that we were not above making the effort to explain our agenda. Such examples may appear trivial, but they demonstrated a willingness to reach out to the other party and get to know them. This is pretty fundamental if you plan to build partnership.

At the time I joined ADL, the GMB had recently elected a new convenor, who had been in the business for some 16 years at the time. Our decision to make him full-time was a clear signal that there was much work to do. In January 1996 I visited him and his shop stewards in their meeting room. The room was a dump. It was damp, poorly lit, with no heating and broken furniture. It was also in the middle of nowhere and took me a long time to find. One of my first actions was to move them into better accommodation with proper facilities, including a PC with e-mail. That's what I mean about dignity and respect. Treat people the way you want to be treated, make their life better and you have the beginnings of a relationship.

'Walk before you can run'?

There will be times when you know the answer but others cannot see it. It is then that you are advised to take stock and try an alternative approach to explain what you mean. The secret is to keep it simple. Try and put yourself in their position and use others as sounding boards to discuss your ideas.

To give an example, one of the shop stewards made a statement to me in June 1996 that made me stop in my tracks and go back to the drawing board. I can still remember it: *'We understand IR, not HR.'* He made it clear that we were trying to be too sophisticated, to run before we could walk. Patience has never been one of my virtues and I was very much aware that the competition was pulling away. On this occasion, however, he was right. We were introducing techniques that the business was not prepared for. Before you launch into the latest thinking in HR practices and models, remember that not everyone reads the same books as you do and that they simply may not understand where you are coming from.

In May that year we had reached a two-year agreement with all three trade unions at a single bargaining table – a first for ADL. We believed that this was a signal that they understood change was both needed and inevitable, but we had read more into their actions than was there. Take care when making assumptions about the strength of relationships; one success does not necessarily mean you have a solid platform to build on.

The June event was designed to create a joint agenda for change. The process was genuinely designed around a 'blank sheet of paper'. Over the course of the day, through managed exercises, we hoped to end up with a formula for change and the items for change. The unions did not believe this, however, and thought we had a change agenda in our 'bottom drawer'.

Furthermore, I could not get the managing director that day so I brought in a film crew and produced a video. The message was again simple – why we had to change and how he was counting on everyone contributing. Yet the MD's failure to attend somehow conveyed a message of lack of importance. If you plan an event that potentially signals the start of significant change, ensure that you have all key stakeholders present. Plan the event around their availability. We learned this lesson the hard way.

The event was due to start at 9.30am. At 9.40 the AEEU turned up and explained that all they had was a 'listening brief' and that, therefore, if I didn't mind, they would 'sit up the back and observe'. This was enough for the GMB to make the same request and send the rest of the participants into absolute confusion. At 9.50am both unions requested an adjournment. I objected: 'How can you have an adjournment from a workshop?' I explained we had arranged a number of exercises and planned breakout sessions and that the day, in fact, had been scheduled to the minute. My pleas were ignored and they left.

At 12.00 noon, they returned and proclaimed they were happy to listen to what we had to say and requested we provide them with a copy of our agenda. As I said, we didn't have one. We did have a list of inefficiencies and examples of 'better practice' rather than best practice. At the end of the day we agreed that we could not stand still and that we had to change to secure any meaningful future. We agreed, therefore, that we would split off our discussions and that all parties would separately pull together their agenda for change.

So what were the lessons from our June workshop? These can be summarised as follows:

- ❧ HR practitioners can be too sophisticated for their own good – keep it simple.
- ❧ Be clear about what you hope to achieve from the event.
- ❧ Explain what you are planning and looking for in the form of an outcome before the event takes place.
- ❧ Make sure all key stakeholders are represented and ideally in attendance.
- ❧ People need support, time and encouragement, not pressure, to come up with ideas.

Achieving buy-in

When stakeholders design the future in partnership, it is very difficult for them to object when it becomes reality. By getting them involved you have already secured some form of buy-in and commitment. If any objections are raised, and they often are, it is easy to respond by saying: 'What's the issue? It was your idea, after all.' This is a tactic I have used a lot. In August 1996 I had all the stakeholders, managers and trade unions present their own recommendations.

Achieving a breakthrough

‘By taking responsibility, people cannot help but get involved’

Building partnership requires some degree of risk. You have to hand over ownership and responsibility to others but retain enough control to ensure that the show does not go off the rails. By taking responsibility, people cannot help but get involved. It's amazing what a difference it makes to personal confidence and pride. The progress we made at ADL became the achievement of the people of ADL.

The watershed event in ADL was what we called the Change Agenda, which I explained in some detail in Chapter 4. It was also a good example of how to build partnership. Having secured the buy-in from Allied Domecq, we focused on the other key stakeholders. In October 1996 we met with union officials and convenors and discussed what we were planning. The officials stressed that we must 'get people to raise their eyes and look at the bigger picture'. We took this on board and focused much of the communication on the threats from the competition and what life could look like for everyone in the company.

Following an enormous amount of detailed preparation by HR and operations management (see Chapter 4), the next task was to enter into detailed negotiations with the unions. We agreed with the union officials that they would make themselves available until we had reached agreement.

The management team was multidisciplined and this improved the quality of our preparation and negotiations. We had created this team some months before the event and rehearsed our arguments until we could recite them without notes. The team remained together not only through the planning and negotiation stage but continued to function (along with the union stewards) during the period we took delivery of each of the change items. I have seen many examples where stakeholders caught up in the emotion of reaching a deal forget that the hard work is actually about taking delivery.

This negotiation process was revolutionary for ADL and helped build relationships between management and employees while both sides produced a comprehensive and detailed document listing the change items over the next three years. During this critical period from 1996 to 1997 we ensured that all employees were engaged. We were determined to involve the line managers, not just the senior executives or the shop floor and trade unions. Too often the middle layer feels excluded and this is one reason why change programmes fail (see Chapter 2 for more details on this point).

We had gone into the discussions with a small document aimed at securing buy-in for the change process. Our recommendation was that following agreement in principle, we would set up joint management/union teams on the earlier model of the local groups. These were departmental teams put in place to implement change. The detail would be worked out by the local groups over the first few months and then implemented. This was unacceptable to the unions, who made it clear that they 'could not sell' an approach based on a blank sheet of paper. They needed the detail. In effect, the trade union forced management to raise their game.

By week two we had more management personnel at the negotiations than unions. We agreed to split up the various tasks and arranged small joint groups to take responsibility for specific areas of change. Each group had complete freedom to research and recommend solutions to recognised problems. In one group the AEEU convenor took the initiative and visited the competition. He came back with detailed plans on multi-skilling engineers that we adopted and ultimately implemented. Other groups followed this example and sought out organisations for solutions to our problems. This had the real benefit of making clear to the unions that management was prepared to listen to ideas and work in partnership.

By the end of week two we had revolutionised ADL – at least on paper. The agreement was comprehensive and covered new terms and conditions, new shift patterns, new systems of working, a description of the typical day and new manning levels, including a planned reduction of 233 people on a voluntary basis. We also extended our non-compulsory redundancy clause for a further two years, assuring every employee that they could stay with ADL if they wanted to. There are not many businesses that offer a guarantee of employment, but over the years we have continued to renew this guarantee.

For the first time, at the insistence of the HR team, management actually sought employees' opinions and involved them directly in shaping the activities and decisions that would improve the company's performance. The Change Agenda created an environment within which it was possible to propose and achieve change in all areas of ADL. By the end of 1997, for example, production line efficiencies – now measured on electronic score cards visible to the whole factory – rose from an average of 55 per cent to over 80 per cent.

Despite such radical changes in performance, none of which would have been achieved without the huge involvement of all our people, the 'softer' measures also moved in the right direction. The annual employee attitude survey showed:

◆ higher morale
◆ greater employee satisfaction
◆ greater personal confidence
◆ increased pride in the business
◆ confirmation that people 'felt safer'.

In the Change Agenda I set out to capture a vision of the future. Much of it we created at ADL but there were elements that I took over from my previous experience at Laura Ashley. The key principles that could work in any business include:

- ❖ We aim to treat each other as adults and to act accordingly.
- ❖ Employees will have a meaningful say in the operation of the business and in decision-making that will influence their work and their lives.
- ❖ We are dedicated to empowerment by ensuring that we have the right person in the right job, clear objectives, regular feedback on performance, education and development. Recognition and reward will be commensurate with achievement and value to the organisation, not necessarily based on status, hierarchy or hours worked.
- ❖ We will develop a flexible approach to work, encompassing remuneration, education, employment practice and the family.
- ❖ We will recognise and value the difference perspectives of a diverse workforce by maintaining an open and unprejudiced working environment that respects the dignity of every employee.
- ❖ We will develop an attitude in all employees where they recognise the impact of their action on customer service and a philosophy where they treat the business as their business.
- ❖ The trade unions will become a social partner with management and will become a source of ideas and inspiration.

Through the implementation of these principles we created a new culture and, in some ways, a new business. The bedrock on which we built this was partnership with our employees. If you want a real breakthrough in your company's performance, you need to tap into the biggest resource you have: the ability, imagination and enthusiasm of your people. Find the hook that obtains their buy-in.

Partnership – put to the test

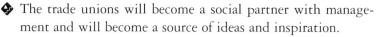

Over time, involvement evolved into influence at ADL. Not only shop stewards but ordinary employees were invited to planning meetings to determine what would be produced on the line that day. We regularly sent people at all levels of the business abroad with the buying team to meet with the manufacturers and suppliers of new equipment. During our busy period from August to December, we would supplement our headcount by employing as many as 200 additional people. We gave the task of recruitment to the unions. We drew up the person specification, determined the number required and reminded them of the legislation. They did not let us down once.

Having said all this, there will still be times when partnership is put to the test. The secret is to keep talking. The role of the HR team is to ensure both parties remain fixed on the vision of what you are trying to achieve. They must keep the show on the road, while challenging the status quo and the robustness of proposals. Once proven, however, HR must play their part in driving through improvements for the benefit of all stakeholders. You also need the patience of a saint.

Partnership at ADL was put to the test a number of times. The most challenging, however, was the maturation review. By late 1997 we were aware that the maturation units were failing to match the improvements in productivity shown elsewhere in the business. We had three primary units called Westthorn, Dumbuck and Willowyard, located in the central belt of Scotland but isolated from the centre of activities in Dumbarton. They were in essence large warehouses where we would lay down casks of whisky for up to 30 years. Yet these were crucial to the production process as it was here we selected the cases needed to produce the different mixtures for our wide range of Scotch whiskies. Most of the work was manual but required great dexterity in moving the huge weights around.

Employees had enjoyed an 18 per cent increase in earnings with the implementation of the Change Agenda, but management were not seeing anything like the same levels in performance improvement. The request for a comprehensive review came from the human resources function. I sat with the production manager and produced the terms of reference for the review and, with the approval of the ADL board, commissioned a consultant to assess performance and recommend areas for improvement.

We had already carried out five similar reviews. Our presentation to the employees and the union was based on those we had used with the other reviews: our joint objective was to become 'best in class' and our belief was that maturation was a major stumbling block to achieving this. We pulled together a joint working party comprising the local middle managers, the shop steward from each area and the HR manager (whose task was to act as facilitator while ensuring that progress was made). The group was tasked with benchmarking our performance and, if shown to be lacking, coming up with recommendations to improve. It was to report each month to a steering committee consisting of directors of the company, senior managers and shop stewards.

As expected, the consultants confirmed there was a huge gap between our performance and the rest of the sector. Their status as independent third-party specialists brought a degree of authority to the process. They validated information we had gathered and their findings largely went unchallenged, which helped speed the change process up.

Given the unique relationship we had with the competition, our own group had the opportunity to visit their workplaces and assess how they were performing against a predetermined checklist. (I accept that this may be difficult to replicate in other sectors, but we did not always have these links. Using networking skills, I set out to establish working relationships with my counterparts in the competition. This was not partnership, but we were prepared to share information provided it did not compromise either party.)

Having gathered their own evidence, the joint working group confirmed the consultants' results and added that, of the units they had visited, ADL was bottom of the league table. Despite this conclusion, however, it took many months to convince the people of Dumbuck, Westthorn and Willowyard that we could and must improve. Every objective had to be dealt with almost line by line. Arguments about safety, stress, layout, equipment, training, structure and so on all had to be addressed. As in previous reviews, we thought it better for people to come with us rather than for management to force through change.

The HR team ensured that they remained impartial (and were seen to be impartial) by assessing both sides of any potential areas of conflict and advising on the best course of action, always considering the long-term benefit. Often issues of great significance to the unions were much less so to management when the bigger picture of cultural change and improved performance was considered. HR took on the task of pointing this out while constantly reminding the group that the issue was a joint problem and therefore needed to be solved jointly.

> ‘Whatever the issue is,
> regardless of how trivial you
> think it is, deal with it quickly’

On a number of occasions partnership was severely put to the test. Scheduled two-hour meetings would take all day. A key lesson was not to let any frustrations fester. Whatever the issue is, regardless of how trivial you think it is, deal with it quickly. HR was instrumental in ensuring that no one lost the drive to succeed.

Having explored all possible options, the working group came up with some courageous and radical recommendations. They argued the need for new equipment, major changes in working practices, the introduction of team leaders and inter-site flexibility. Each of these was to be supported by a new warehouse management system. These recommendations transformed productivity and performance and led to substantial savings. The average rate rose from 2.8 casks per man hour in 1998 to 9.2 by December 1999. Even more radically, the working group proposed a new manning level, resulting in a staff reduction of over 50 per cent.

Partnership with employees and the community

As must already be clear, partnership developed from dealing mainly with the unions to encouraging all our people to get involved. The 'nine box' matrix described in Chapter 5 (Fig. 12) rewarded behaviours that reinforced the culture we were trying to create as well as the achievement of personal objectives. We introduced high-visibility 'key results areas', personal objectives at all levels and gainsharing schemes that aligned every employee's activities behind the business targets and strategy. We invested £2.5 million on training. In the first 12 months we devoted 31,000 hours to up-skilling and multi-skilling alone.

The result was a growing feeling among employees that the company was theirs. They were happy to volunteer to take the lead in presentations and let anyone know what they had achieved. Ordinary employees would be asked to attend corporate events normally restricted to senior managers and customers. Invitations to the Edinburgh Tattoo, Scottish Ballet, Scottish Cup Finals and international rugby games, for example, gave them a chance to mix with key customers and politicians.

In 1999 and 2000 we set out to build stronger links with local people. We were determined to get across what our plans would mean for employment in the Dumbarton area for years to come. We also targeted 13 members of the Scottish Parliament who represented areas where we had units so as to make them aware of what we were doing. Many visited Kilmalid. The leader of the Scottish Parliament, the late Donald Dewar, took part in the 'topping out' ceremony and his successor Henry McLeish formally opened the completed building in April 2001. We visited the Scottish Parliament and told our story there. When I say 'we', it was HR, ordinary employees and shop stewards.

We also targeted the business community. HR designed a conference promoting 'best in class' ideas. This idea was sold to the CBI at Centre Point in London and, under its banner of 'Fit for the future', we and CBI Scotland organised and ran an event that over 100 Scottish business leaders attended. As expected, ADL focused on partnership. Our managing director hosted the full day, and the profit we made from the event was given to local charities. Few of these initiatives count as mainstream HR activities, yet at ADL they were all designed and introduced by the HR team.

How do you sustain partnership?

In summary, I would stress the following:

- ❖ Make time for people, since patience *is* a virtue.
- ❖ Solve problems quickly – don't let them fester.
- ❖ Over time grow involvement into true influencing.
- ❖ Give everyone the opportunity to shape the strategy of the business.
- ❖ Jointly celebrate success.
- ❖ Recognise people at all levels for their achievements.
- ❖ When you fall out – kiss and make up.

Summary

Partnership is built on trust, personal integrity and mutual respect. If any of these is missing from either party, partnership will fail. Effective communication is, therefore, a must. In 1995, the focus was on building a better relationship with the unions and our employees. Since then we have taken positive action to build partnership with suppliers, local people and the business community. The techniques are the same.

It's about doing what you say and keeping your promises. This also implies that everyone has a voice that is valued. This can only be achieved by both encouraging and maximising involvement. By building stronger relationships with employees and recognising they are stakeholders who would welcome the opportunity to shape the direction of the business, you are building an organisation that others will find difficult to copy – and that's a differential advantage. Partnership can make a bottom-line difference.

Chapter 7

HR strategy and business strategy

Clive Morton

The logic is compelling. Human resources strategy should be inextricably linked with business strategy. HR should understand and align with business language – otherwise, what's the point of considering HR's best contribution? The evidence of the link between human resource management and the bottom line has been increasingly made evident in recent years. Yet industry in general is still not applying people practices to any great extent.

What about HR strategy? Is it, as some would see it, about implementing the people implications of others' business strategy? Or is it about shaping the business of tomorrow?

Business strategy itself has gone through a transformation in recent decades, from the extrapolation of numbers in strategic planning to the wider contextually based scenarios so popular today. The range of options is enormous, from blue skies to the more certain benchmark comparisons with known experience. Also, businesses need different HR interventions at different stages of the growth cycle.

To me the issue is one of proactivity. Is HR on the front foot with strategy – its own and in relation to business strategy? Or is it waiting in the wings to be told what is required for the next move? Being proactive has to be tempered with a strong sense of business need. Having a wonderful concept that cannot be implemented is just as ineffective as being reactive and not contributing to strategy.

Andrew and Jon demonstrate a keen understanding of the place of strategy, which is as much about the timing of interventions as the use of strategy itself.

The term 'HR strategy' has come in recently for outright attack. Professor Amin Rajan, in a hard-hitting report entitled *Tomorrow's Organisation: New mindsets, new skills*, calls HR strategy a vacuously empty term. The results of research carried out by CREATE for the London Human Resource Group show that the term 'strategic HR' covers different activities depending upon where an organisation is in its life cycle (for details of this see list on pages 134–5). Amin Rajan argues that:

> Strategic HR is not an immutable concept. It needs to be considered in relation to the life cycle of the organisation and changing priorities in a fluid environment. Currently, there is too much hype around this concept: unless it is defined in a dynamic context, it is an empty concept.[1]

In this Amin Rajan recognises the changing concept of business strategy in general:

> Not long ago, the term strategy had a very clear meaning in financial, professional and business services: it covered tactics and actions to achieve clearly articulated business goals. As such, it had a military connotation. However, in the fluid environment of the last five years, when the goalposts have been shifting unpredictably, it no longer is possible to have rigid goals ...
>
> Strategy is about building the capability to cope with an ever-changing environment. Not only is it influenced by overt business processes and actions. But it is also influenced by intangibles like culture, ideology and leadership within individual organisations. Equally important, they vary over the life cycle of an organisation.
>
> Like humans, organisations go through three clear phases of evolution: growth, maturity and decline. But that's where the similarity ends. For organisations have one advantage. They can initiate the fourth stage: *renewal*. Great companies of today have been through successive phases of renewals over time, in ways that are not yet possible for us humans![2]

This reflects the graduation from what we know as strategic planning to strategic thinking.

Henry Mintzberg pioneered much of the concept in his seminal book *The Rise and Fall of Strategic Planning*, saying that strategic planning is a contradiction in terms, an unhelpful oxymoron like 'fun run', 'friendly fire' and 'military intelligence'. Mintzberg quotes a favourite philosopher of mine, Kierkegaard – 'Life may be lived forward, but it is understood backwards.'[3]

‹If business strategy has to be fluid, then so must HR strategy›

What does this mean in terms of HR's best contribution?

It must be that there is no 'set' HR contribution – no one formula or one size fits all. It must be that if business strategy has to be fluid, then so must HR strategy. Whereas this is perfectly logical, it also feeds the vulnerability of HRM justification's being dependent on past evidence – based on a past context that may not apply now. Hence advocates of the 'best practice' school are peddling solutions for problems that might be yesterday's issues, not necessarily those of today.

The overriding factor of this book is that of HR leadership. It is the crucial role of leaders in the HR context that makes a difference. Followers can apply best practice and it may work. HR leaders know the toolkit but have the ability to judge where and when to apply it, or indeed when to create new tools for new situations. No wonder Dave Ulrich of Michigan University terms them HR champions. This makes the connection with the enormous contributions from Jon and Andrew in their organisations and in demonstrating in this book how HR can make the difference.

Can we bridge the divide?

HR strategy and business strategy have been parallel, different and mainly unconnected. Business strategy has been related to models of financial and business growth: concepts based on market, customer analysis, market entry and competitive forces. Having established the model, the policy and strategy, then the strategists got round to dealing with the resource question. We know what we need – just a matter of find, afford, deploy – what's the problem?

The HR strategy school said we must find the right formula for attraction, motivation and retention; then we've solved the resource problem. Some good theory, frameworks and practices emerged, but often in isolation from the thinking on business strategy. Business changed direction and the HR strategy was left floating like an ice floe on turbulent water. HR strategy needs to move from the back foot to the leading edge – influencing and combining with business strategy.

For survival and growth today, the antennae of business has to be so good and all in the business have to participate in understanding and analysing trends. This is the real challenge for HR strategy – to contribute beyond HR administration and employee relations, and change into steering the business using the intellectual capital within and with other connected organisations outside.

'Culture change creates a unique competitive advantage,' says Dave Ulrich. This sounds very fluffy to the hard-nosed. What does it mean? Is it true? To work it has to loop back to the need for agility in organisations. If the culture won't allow invention, imagination, cross-functional dialogue and learning, then there is little chance of sustainable competitive advantage – little chance of agility and speed of response to customer needs. Culture change is a people product, an enabler that needs to be owned by the whole business, not just enthusiastic HR professionals. This means convincing the peer group as well as the CEO – a test of the skills of persuasion.

The biggest cracks show between business strategy and HR strategy in the mergers and acquisitions (M&A) crucible. HR is not at the M&A table as of right. Finance and Legal have a reserved place at the table. HR has to earn its place. The fact that 80 per cent of M&A activity fails to enhance shareholder value and that the majority of failures are due to people and culture problems seems to be cheerfully ignored.

Lastly, what is employer brand? Is it something that HR can formulate? Or a reflected glory from marketing? We know it is a crucial factor in attracting, retaining and motivating key talent. We also know that the external brand needs to dovetail with the internal brand. The strategies to achieve employer of choice are explored in depth by Jon in Chapter 9.

Why does the evidence of people strategies not lead to more application?

In *Beyond World Class* (Macmillan 1998) I concluded that:

❖ People management practices can give 20 per cent productivity and profit improvement compared to 6 per cent from a combination of R&D, innovation and quality.[4]

❖ Maintaining effective trust *relationships* and communication (voice) with suppliers and employees flows through to consistently higher productivity and profits.

❖ Agility of organisations is a function of a culture of learning and change within – *speed of response* going beyond quality, cost and delivery.

❖ Those companies that are *inclusive* in their relationships inside and with their communities stay the course, are consistently more profitable and more able to make strategic choices for the future.

❖ Those companies that exploit *total quality systems* to the full outperform the marketplace in every sense.

❖ Leading companies are those who *live with ambiguity and deal effectively with dilemmas* such as short term and long term, control and autonomy, and so on.

All of these are added to other parallel evidence, giving HR professionals just the information they need to show that HRM really does make the difference.

However, the disappointing result is that industry in general (whether private or public sectors) is still not applying people practices to any great extent. David Guest finds:[5]

Convincing evidence to support this claim comes from two new studies. The first is the authoritative government-sponsored Workplace Employee Relations Survey. This survey of almost 2,200 workplaces covering all sectors of industry asked lots of questions about human resource practices. A list of 17 key practices covering all the main aspects of human resource management was generated. Of 1,278 private-sector establishments employing 25 or more, only 21 per cent have more than half the practices in place. Only 16 per cent have four or less in place. Among the 546 public-sector work-places, 35 per cent had more than half in place. The private sector, where one might expect to see a more advanced form of human resource management, seems to be lagging behind.

A slightly more positive picture comes from a second study, funded by the ESRC as part of its Future of Work programme with additional support from the CIPD. In a sample of 610 private-sector organisations employing 50 or more, and using an overlapping list of 17 practices, 57 per cent had more than half in place.

David Guest puts forward a number of plausible explanations of why the message about HRM and performance is not hitting home:[6]

1   *The message is not being heard by personnel managers.* There is no evidence to suggest that more human resource practices are applied in workplaces where more sophisticated personnel management is in place.

2   *The message is not believed.* Investment in human resources and human resource practices does not fit a culture that emphasises cost control. For some, the suggestion that people management is a more important determinant of financial performance than R&D, new technology and business strategy is treated as frankly incredible.

3   *Personnel managers believe the message but cannot sell it.* While this may have been a plausible explanation in the past, it seems increasingly untenable. It would therefore appear to be a good time to sell HRM in organisations.

4   *Personnel managers don't know how to introduce HRM.* There is a history of seeking 'quick hits' in areas like the use of competencies or performance-related pay. These can have a positive impact but only if they are part of a coherent strategy, and all too often this is not the case. Where HRM is carefully applied, with competent, supportive management and an appropriate management culture, it can have a positive impact.

5   *Personnel managers are too busy managing turbulence and change to develop a sustained human resource strategy.* With organisational change and uncertainty rife in organisations, the search for consistency may appear unrealistic.

6   *Academic messages are muddled and contradictory.* While some researchers are advocating the use of 'high commitment' or 'high performance' work practices in all organisations, others argue that there is strategic choice. Those organisations operating in a

> 'black hole' where there is no union representation and little or
> no progressive human resource management are likely to have
> poor employment relations, low commitment, poorer quality of
> work and higher labour turnover and absence.

All of these explanations have validity in differing circumstances,
but for me the crucial issues are 3–5 above, which are about leadership and establishing priorities – coming back to the critical
role of HR leadership! I find it fascinating to compare this list of
explanations (or excuses) against the clear experience of Jon and
Andrew in their chapters that leadership and intervention work in
achieving for business and people.

A further intuition can be added to this list – that of half-hearted
implementation or the difference between rhetoric and reality.
Too many organisations have seen faddism or a chase after the
latest fashion giving rise to poor or inappropriate implementation, 'initiativitis' and subsequent failure, feeding cynicism and
resistance to change.

HR strategy is situational

‘Strategy is contextual and related to the life cycle of organisations’

Professor Amin Rajan concludes in *Tomorrow's Organisation* –
based on a survey of 247 organisations in seven industries in the
financial, professional and business services sector – that HR
strategy has to be situational. In other words, strategy is contex-
tual and related to the life cycle of organisations.

Changing HR priorities over the organisational life cycle
Key preoccupations in each phase of the organisational life cycle
are listed below:

♦ *Phase 1: Growth:*
  ♦ recruitment
  ♦ payroll and administration

- training and development
- promotions
- compensation and benefits
- transfers.

- *Phase 2: Maturity:*
  - succession planning
  - legislation
  - communication
  - performance management
  - staff survey
  - flexible working.

- *Phase 3: Decline:*
  - mergers and acquisitions
  - benchmarking
  - evaluation
  - rationalisation
  - exit management.

- *Phase 4: Renewal:*
  - culture change
  - leadership development
  - business re-engineering
  - retention
  - motivation
  - coaching and mentoring
  - employer brand
  - employee champion
  - talent management
  - knowledge management.[7]

However, the emerging models of HR organisations in the study typically apply to companies who have reached either the maturity phase or the decline phase but are now trying to stage a renewal. Hence for start-up companies it is bound to be different, so Jon's experiences in Generics probably require a different model, whereas the dominant preoccupation in other studies in this book is one of changing existing organisations. The common solution in the emerging models is to converge the roles of HR professionals and line managers.

Amin Rajan finds:[8]

❖ A partnership is evolving under which HR professionals are getting involved in issues that directly impact on business; line managers, in turn, are increasingly taking on an operational role.

❖ In part, all these developments are driven by cost considerations, although the projected savings are not notable; the figures reported in the media typically do not discount the investment in systems, external consultancy support in the transitional phase and redundancy costs.

❖ The real aim is to raise the effectiveness of the HR organisation to make a positive contribution to corporate renewal and success.

While it might be a logical trend if we say that HR strategy must integrate with business strategy, in practice it is a concept that needs very proactive support. It is very clear from David Guest's list that proactive leadership from HR is needed to make it happen. Although I would always want the line directors and managers involved, it must be seen as enthusiastic ownership, not yet another onerous, unwanted task dumped on over-pressed managers.

The HR strategist in practice

The beauty of the opportunity in this book is to relate the frameworks, theory and survey results of others to what is really happening in leading-edge situations. Both Jon and Andrew have achieved in the school of hard knocks, overcoming many of the obstacles we have identified.

Both clearly show the importance of leadership – the HR professional must know both *how* to lead and, more importantly, *when* to lead (and when to support or facilitate when others should lead).

Taking **Jon's story** in Chapter 3, we can see the importance of proactive support in integrating HR strategy with business strategy. The aim here is not to show *what* the particular HR strategy was (as we've seen, there is no 'one size fits all'), rather *how* it was that Jon and his team moved onto the front foot and ensured that the views of the HR function were heard and contributed to business goals.

The HR function, and the HR strategy, will get nowhere near the table at which key business decisions are being made, and strategy set, unless they are credible. Jon points out essential key attributes that enable HR to gain credibility:

◆ a depth of understanding of the business context
◆ exceptional analytical skills
◆ highly developed political and diplomatic capability
◆ sensitivity and insight.

However, this skill set is not in itself enough to ensure inclusion – it must be backed up by proof of performance. The efficiency and quality of the day-to-day activities have an impact on the bottom line and are vital in showing credibility. No high-flying strategy is possible unless there is a solid base of effective and speedy administration – which is so easily destroyed by carelessness (I have a memory etched on my mind of a CEO receiving his long-service certificate through the post with the glass broken and the frame cracked!).

From this comes another lesson on credibility: it is hard to gain, but is easily lost. As a result, the HR practitioner *must* deliver on the promises that he or she makes. We as a profession are not yet considered as other functions of the business who see that they have a position at the strategy table as of right. Great steps have been made, but we have to keep delivering if we are to keep the forward momentum.

Jon also sees a crucial role in today's networked organisation of HR creating and managing the soft glue that binds, aligns and motivates – in effect HR operating a networked role inside and outside the organisation (formal professional accreditation doesn't teach this!). This makes cohesive sense of HRM in the business context. The perspective that the function has on the world outside the company is unique and this should feed directly into business goals.

These last two points also serve to highlight the importance of forging strong relationships: with peers, the CEO, heads of functions and 'beyond the factory gates', with the added value of being ambassador as HR gets involved outside.

Finally, any proactive role must give consideration to the interventions that may need to be made. As we have seen, the timing of the interventions are often as important as the strategy itself. So for Jon, the opportunity to draft the business principles of spin-out was a 'natural job for the head of HR'. We also see a role in challenging and supporting the line. As Jon notes: 'It is the role of HR today to challenge the line. This is not always comfortable, isn't the best approach to making friends and is never easy, but it is our job. In the long term we satisfy the long-term needs of the business.'

Andrew's story in Chapter 4 focuses on the other key issue that will invariably be found when aligning business and HR strategies: change management – in this case, warts and all. This was not a situation where long-term planning or starting from scratch with a clean sheet of paper was possible. This is the HR professional in at the deep end with a wave machine producing new challenges all the time (rather akin to item 5 in the list of obstacles highlighted by David Guest earlier in this chapter).

This shows the HR function making clear decisions on when and when not to take the lead, while all the time remaining proactive. For example, the use of more junior employees to deliver the change message shows the HR function leading from the very front. All the key events were planned and executed by the HR team and had direct business benefit. This was not a support function, but a function that led! In contrast, Andrew saw the HR role as facilitation, not leadership – however, this didn't preclude a decisive intervention, such as over the in-house tankering bid. It is uncanny, but that sequence was followed stage by stage by the successful in-house bid for tankering in Anglian Water four years ago against fierce external competition – with a similar HR role of facilitation.

The story is one of success; the team effectively overturned decades of history and fulfilled the organisation's dream of becoming 'best in class'. Not surprisingly, there are a number of points from this story that serve well as a checklist for anyone involved in the process of culture change at the point where alignment is taking place:

❧ *A focus on culture and the determination to do something about it* – the use of measurement in this area is powerful. Andrew talks of comparing the culture measures across sites and with best in class – this is similar to my experience in a number of organisations. It very effectively holds a mirror up to an organisation, showing them where they are and helping *them* to chart a journey to a new performance culture.

❧ *An understanding that strategic decisions* – in this case to move all staff on to the Kilmalid site – *give the opportunity of creating a new culture.*

❧ *For culture change to be effective the whole orchestra has to be used and to be in tune!* For instance, the use of effective written communications inside and out; that top-down communication on its own isn't enough; 14 channels of communications; a human face on directors; involving external influencers – MPs, ministers, trade union officials and lastly, like Jon's example, Andrew presented the external face of the organisation to the wider community.

❧ *The need for HR professionals to be change agents* who can, in Andrew's words, 'paint a vision of what life will look like tomorrow and ensure that the business gets there.'

In order to achieve any of the above, the HR function quickly realised that they had to help build trust down the organisation and at the same time sell the change agenda upwards – using the data and anticipation of power and reaction. Andrew's trust and confidence in people shines through.

Despite these successes, Andrew demonstrates another key ability: to learn from your mistakes. As the Project STAR showed, the introduction of a best-practice solution without strategy alignment is no more than a solution for somebody else's problem. Failure of a project like this always makes it more difficult to implement the subsequent and real solutions. However, all will not be lost as long as you learn the lesson, and learn it well.

The message that we are left with is clear:

> The challenge for HR was not so much the 'change management' element in itself, but the demands of dealing with a large number of changes going on at the same time.

Conclusions on HR strategy and business strategy

‹HR strategy and business strategy need context for definition – it is situational and dependent on change›

It is clear that HR strategy and business strategy need context for definition – it is situational and dependent on change. Hence leadership and intervention is needed to get the focus right and to seize the opportunity.

The divide in schools of thought that affects business strategy inevitably affects the HR version. In Chapter 2 on sustainability, I argue for a double-loop approach that should balance external and internal influences on learning. Hamel and Prahalad's[9] notion of the core competence of a firm suggests that firms should build their strategies to what they do best (sticking to the knitting). Professor Wayne Brockbank,[10] however, points out that this condemns a firm's strategic thinking to a short-term perspective. He argues that, 'what counts are not the core technical competencies but the core cultural competencies: the key competence, however, is not what a firm does based on what is known, but is, rather, a firm having a culture which encourages flexibility, change, learning creativity and adaptability to customers.'

Linda Holbeche in *Aligning Human Resources and Business Strategy*[11] challenges HR practitioners to identify the future organisation needs via such questions as:

❖ What will the competitive marketplace for the company's products, services and labour look like over the next five to 10 years?
❖ What is the company's core competence, especially over the next three to five years?
❖ What kind of human resources will the organisation need in order to compete successfully, or to continue to develop and provide high-quality services?
❖ What types of HR practices are relevant to building the organisation needed for the future?

What this is about is forward vision based on shared values – not just coping with today.

Summary

♣ Effective HR strategy is as much about timing as it is an understanding of business need.

♣ The HR leader must know all the tools in the 'best practice toolkit' *and* know when and where to apply them or not.

♣ There is overwhelming evidence supporting the importance of HRM to the bottom line, yet effective people practices are not being widely implemented. It is for the HR practitioner to take this evidence and champion the practices within the business.

♣ HR strategy has to be situational; there is no 'one size fits all'. Among other factors, the strategy will be determined by the organisation's stage in life: growth, maturity, decline, renewal.

♣ In order to have an impact on business strategy, the HR function *must* be credible. This can only be achieved through performance and by delivering on the promises that you make.

♣ Change will not be successful without a complete understanding of the relationship between change strategy (and therefore HR strategy) and business strategy.

References

1 RAJAN A. (2001) *Tomorrow's Organisation: New mindsets, new skills.* Tunbridge Wells, CREATE. p28.

2 *Ibid.* p27.

3 MINTZBERG H. (1993) *The Rise and Fall of Strategic Planning.* London, Prentice-Hall Europe.

4 PATTERSON M., WEST M., LAWTHOM R. *and* NICKELL S. (1997) *Impact of People Management Practices on Business Performance.* London, Institute of Personnel and Development.

5 GUEST D. (1999) *People Strategies for Competitive Success.* Paper presented to IPD National Conference. Guest's research in this area is ongoing; those interested should consult the CIPD's publications.

6 *Ibid.*

7 RAJAN A. (2001) *Tomorrow's Organisation: New mindsets, new skills.* Tunbridge Wells, CREATE. p28.

8 *Ibid.* pp38–9.

9 HAMEL G. *and* PRAHALAD C. K. (1994) *Competing for the Future.* Boston, Mass., Harvard Business School Press.

10 BROCKBANK W. (1997) 'HR's future on the way to a presence'. *Human Resource Management.* Vol. 36, No. 1. Spring.

11 HOLBECHE L. (1999) *Aligning Human Resources and Business Strategy.* London, Butterworth-Heinemann. Reprinted by permission of Butterworth-Heinemann.

Chapter 8

Operating at board level

Jon Sparkes

Business context of HR strategy

In Chapter 3 I referred to becoming a business partner: the aim of the HR function and the human resources professional for a number of years. This chapter takes this a step further: it looks at HR operating at board level in today's organisation.

Clive has already described the tangle of issues faced by organisations today, both internally and externally, and Andrew has described the fundamental role of HR in managing change, building partnership and enabling organisational learning. This chapter builds on these factors. Operating at board level is about both converting the business context into HR strategy, policies, practice and procedures, and converting HR, labour market and cultural realities into clear business strategy and context.

Any attempt to describe or make observations about HR operating at board level clearly goes right to the heart of the role of the board in today's company. Long gone are the days of strict hierarchy and the role of the board being to determine strategy and policy on behalf of the owners and pass it down – the organisation no longer works in a nice, neat one-dimensional hierarchy. There are regulatory, statutory, ethical and best practice matters to be considered. There is a plethora of stakeholders. The external context has gone global. Culture and other people issues have found their way to the centre of the corporate agenda.

I will go on to consider the question of what the HR director does all day. Immediately prior to joining the board of Scientific Generics, one of my team asked me what would be different. This chapter tells what is different, and what might be different now I have joined the board of the Generics Group shortly after flotation on the London Stock Exchange. It will demonstrate the range of issues that prey on the mind of the HR professional operating at board level.

‹HR strategy must get to grips with the impact of external questions and internal needs›

Looking at the role of HR at board level also requires us to examine the question of HR strategy. This must be more than a big resourcing, development and reward plan. The HR strategy must get to grips with the impact of external questions of business climate and economy and the internal needs of the future business in terms of such aspects as culture, vitality, dynamism, change orientation, volatility, openness, risk profile and structure as well as the numbers, the core competencies, the skills profile, the rewards equation and so on. This area is dealt with in greater detail by Clive in Chapter 7, but it is a vital element in giving an overview of the role of HR at the board.

My intention is to understand what we mean when we say HR should be on the board. It isn't enough to point at people being the most important resource and saying therefore that HR should be on the board. If this were so, then everyone would be on the board if they had responsibility for an important resource. We have to point at the contribution HR will make and how this adds value to the company and the people in it. If it's simply day-to-day added value and risk management, then we shouldn't sit at the board. If it really is a strategic function, able to point the way for the company and convert that into tangible business results for all stakeholders, then we might just be fulfilling a board position.

Role of the board in today's organisation
The paradoxes
So what is the role of the board in today's organisation, and how does that have an impact on the HR professional? The best way to answer this question is to look at the following paradoxes:[1]

Paradox one – the board must be entrepreneurial and move the business forward while keeping it under prudent control. In French, entrepreneur means stager of drama. So the board must stage the drama that challenges the business and its assumptions, while maintaining a steadying hand on that business.

 Paradox two – the board must be sufficiently knowledgeable about the workings of the company because it is answerable for its actions, yet must be able to stand back from day-to-day management and retain an objective, longer-term view.

 Paradox three – the board must be sensitive to the pressures of short-term local issues and be informed about, and plan in the context of, broad trends.

 Paradox four – the board is expected to be focused on the commercial needs of the organisation and act responsibly towards employees, partners and society.

Perhaps 'paradox' is too strong a word for describing these tensions. The point is that the board is more than a glorified management team; it has responsibilities beyond the running of the business today to meet today's objectives. It also has to grapple with subjects that seem to contradict. The board as a calm, prudent and objective stager of drama just about sums it up!

For the HR professional operating at board level, we begin to see from these paradoxes both a general role and some areas of particular expertise.

If the business is to move forward, the HR professional must provide the communication channels, the change processes, the understanding of the current situation and the organisation's ability to change, the reward and motivational mechanisms, and the employee development interventions (to name but a few areas of responsibility) to enable the drama to be staged. Not only that, but the HR professional at board level must play a full part in determining the story and writing the script. The HR professional must also ensure that prudence is maintained, both through his or her own areas of responsibility and through cross-board matters of risk management, corporate governance and statutory compliance.

The HR professional at the board must make it his or her business to understand the workings of the company. How many HR people can honestly say that they have done this? When I was looking for my first job, I wanted to move into the arena of employee relations. As I looked at what companies had on offer, I was surprised by the lack of companies who would put their budding employee relations fast-trackers on the shop floor for a stint at the sharp end before allowing them even to join in the back-office support for employee relations management.

If the HR professional sits at the very heart of any of these paradoxes, it is the final one – concentrating on the commercial needs of the company while acting responsibly towards the employees. A good example of this is a previous experience of large-scale redundancies. It is in such circumstances that this paradox reaches its limits. If the commercial needs of the business really do warrant large-scale redundancies, then the ability to be fair towards the employees is tested!

The answer is, of course, to be as fair as possible. The HR professional at the board must insist on early and effective communication, real and meaningful consultation with employees and their representatives, objectivity in decision-making, generosity in severance, assistance in job search, and many other interventions that do not, on the face of it, contribute to the immediate commercial need. This is a stark example, but the HR professional at the board will meet this paradox frequently and will have to operate as both commercially minded director and employee champion.

The mechanics

A more formal description of the role of the board in today's organisation would include the following elements:[2]

❖ determine vision, mission and values of the company
❖ determine strategies and structure
❖ delegate to management
❖ accept responsibilities to stakeholders (shareholders, customers, suppliers, employees, local community etc)

❖ protect achievements
❖ ensure availability of resources.

In short, decision-making, compliance and leadership describe the role of the board. This all seems very simple. The reality is of course very different. For example, the emergence of what Clive describes as the 'self-employed mindset' presents a significant challenge for the board and is of particular concern to the HR professional at the board.

Typical of the knowledge organisations of the early twenty-first century, the Generics Group relies on the availability of highly skilled individuals. One group springs directly to mind, as they currently sit prominently on UK lists of rare skills: the optoelectronic engineers. Generics has to manage the age-old paradox of attracting and retaining them using the very techniques, structures and processes that make them even more marketable. This is a fact, and one that we must respond to by doing those things even more; anything that restricted the development and creation of career opportunities for these people would be an attempt to restrict their mindset flexibility – with immediate negative effect. The business model relies on a supply of excellent people, and they are attracted by:

❖ the prospect of working with equally excellent people
❖ a range of challenging and different projects to work on
❖ investment in their ideas and the opportunity to take their ideas forward
❖ development of both their technical and commercial skills
❖ participation in all aspects of the commercialising of technology, from sales and proposal-writing, through project management and creative laboratory and development work to the final presentation to client or setting up of licensing deal
❖ the opportunity to participate in taking their idea to ultimate fruition through the creation of a new spin-out company
❖ being well paid for the work they enjoy and participating financially in the development of their ideas.

Providing this environment would not traditionally be seen as a recipe for headcount growth. It is *today's* recipe for headcount growth. It is also an example of the sort of issue that should prey on the mind of the board. This is not a matter of recruitment and retention; it is a matter of fundamental importance in satisfying the needs of shareholders, it is a matter of the selling and commercial proposition and process, it is a matter of technology due diligence, asset protection and commercialisation, and it is a matter of organisational strategy and structure. I will return to this recipe in the final chapter on becoming an employer of choice.

This is not a comprehensive description of the role of the board; it merely demonstrates something of the context into which the HR professional enters on joining the board. The board deals with the paradoxes and the HR professional must learn to place himself or herself at the centre of those paradoxes. We need to:

 be the flamboyant and challenging stager of dramas *and* the prudent protector of assets and achievements

 understand the detail of the business (particularly the life experience of the people in and around the business) *and* retain the objective long-term view (particularly of the employment market)

 remain commercially focused *and* be seen within and without the board to be championing responsibility towards employees and other stakeholders.

What the HR director does all day

The HR director is one of a group of people with the responsibility to deal with the paradoxes. This is relatively clear. What might be less clear is how this translates into the day-to-day activities of the HR director.

One of my Loughborough University lecturers, Peter Lawrence, described what managers and directors do all day in his book *Invitation to Management*:[3]

 almost 30 per cent of the general manager's time is spent in formal meetings

 almost 20 per cent is spent in ad hoc informal meetings

❖ almost 20 per cent involves moving around the business (usually participating in even more ad hoc discussions)
❖ almost 10 per cent is spent on the telephone.

In fact, the study shows that only just over 10 per cent of the time is spent doing the manager's own individual work tasks.

This certainly rings true when considering what the HR director does all day. There are five hats that the HR director is expected to wear, and these go some way to explaining the content of all of those meetings and discussions and the value of the 10 per cent personal work time. They are:

❖ employee champion
❖ change manager
❖ custodian of culture
❖ challenger of operational status quo
❖ deliverer of resource.

Employee champion

‹As employee champion, the HR director is interested in understanding how the organisation is "feeling"›

In fulfilling the role that David Ulrich[4] describes as employee champion, the HR director is interested in understanding how the organisation is 'feeling' and the perceptions employees have of how the organisation is being managed and managing itself. Without this information it is difficult to make changes required to ensure that the organisation 'feels' more like it is achieving something and that the perceptions of employees are more positive. The making of such changes needs to be directed at the organisation's strategy, structures and processes, not back at the employees.

So, how do we go about getting credible information? This is not just about employee surveys, but they play a very important role.

They are what psychometric tests are to the gut feel and pop psychology of interviewing. They are the ice on the puddles you point at when a child says that it can't be cold because the sun is shining.

The HR director must spend time, usually in formal meetings and informal discussions ensuring that the rest of the board is bought into the collection of employee perception data. The HR director must be satisfied that the questions are robust, the process for data collection is unambiguous and rigorous, the analysis is impartial and the results communicated more fully.

However, these are not the key elements and do not reflect the majority of the time spent by the HR director. There are three time-consuming aspects:

1 *Really getting to grips with the data* – clearly, someone else may be responsible for compiling and analysing the data, but the HR director needs to know the data – not just the headlines, but the patterns and trends throughout the data. He or she needs to have the analytical ability and interest to spend time studying the data and looking at it in every different way.

2 *Understanding the information* – again, someone else may present the data to the HR director, but he or she must make it his or her business to understand it. This is back to the paradoxes; no one else at the board will spend the same amount of time as the HR director trying to understand why the data is what it is. In other words, the HR director translates for the board.

3 *Communicating and action* – of all of the time the HR director spends on this activity, 95 per cent must be spent communicating, enabling and catalysing the development of action plans and ensuring through whatever means are possible that those plans are implemented. Back to Peter Lawrence's study: the value added by the HR director is in the meetings and the ad hoc discussions, rather than in the desk work.

The best way to obtain information about the state of the organisation and the perceptions of the people is to spend time with the people! And this does not just mean asking fellow directors. The

HR director can be honest broker and devil's advocate in board discussions about the organisation only if he or she has independent sources of information.

At the extreme, when discussing the success or otherwise of – for example – an acquisition, the HR director needs to know what motivation is like in the acquired company and how the expatriate manager of the business is coping with the personal shock of relocating with his or her family to North America. We need to know how the rest of the organisation is integrating with the new company – whether the IT integration is helping, if the sales pipeline management processes have adapted quickly enough and if the newly acquired employees feel they are being communicated with. We can ask those with formal responsibility or we can spend time in the new company and find out over a beer whether things are going as well as people think back at base.

Equally important is the HR director's responsibility to spend time ensuring that this hard and soft information is understood by his or her fellow directors and the HR team. Some of the most valuable time each day is spent with the managing director – when both people are in the office for a day, typically three or four ad hoc meetings of 20 minutes or so will enable a considerable amount of communicating, prioritising and agenda repositioning. This is far more valuable than the monthly or weekly one-to-one, as today's networked and boundaryless organisation rarely fits into such neat calendar cycles. Policy-making and strategic decisions often need to be dealt with in real time.

Similarly, spending time with the finance director will be invaluable. This is the person with the most stark view of the organisation. He or she will not necessarily understand what the customers are thinking today, but will know how everything the company is doing is converting into harsh financial reality. Time spent with the FD is an essential part of the HR director's day. In 10 or 20 minutes we can understand how the city analysts are feeling about the future of the organisation – what is impressing them and where the risks are. It can also give you a spin-free view of where the resourcing hot and cold spots are going to be over the next few months. This time will also help to temper the FD's view of the company, enabling him or her to understand the impact of particular decisions on employee motivation and, ultimately, headcount or staff turnover.

This time is, of course, also the opportunity to do business, for example to put the technical issues relating to the share option scheme for employees in a particular country back to the top of the ever-changing agenda.

Change manager

As change manager, the HR director is looking to move the organisational behaviour from one place to another. This may be in response to external trends or to internal performance issues. This may involve a formal change programme, but will more likely be woven into everyday business.

For example, the following issues from my own work highlight the various attributes of the change manager:

- *Achieving buy-in for a series of board development interventions* — unfailing delivery of growth will not be delivered by each business unit performing better; it will be achieved by the business units working together. Development of the board will not necessarily involve making the individual directors perform better; it must focus on making the team work together more strategically and with greater synergy.
- *The metrics need to be consistent with the new aims of the business and all communication methods need to be used to reinforce this* — the bonus scheme is a strong communication method and the HR director starts with a proposal formulated alongside the FD to be presented to the remuneration committee to ensure that executive directors' bonus arrangements are consistent. Then the bonus arrangements for all staff are formulated; the system is modelled to test the impact of various business scenarios and communicated. The process for managing, assessing and rewarding innovation needs to be made more transparent; the HR director needs to make this his or her business. The impact of the changing metrics needs to be reflected in the

performance management processes, the career development framework, succession planning and many other aspects of the HR mix.

❖ *The resourcing pipeline needs to be even more robust* – a series of meetings with the network of recruitment companies shares with them the hopes for the business and continues to build on these essential relationships. A trip to the USA starts the process of building such a network in Maryland. New ways are devised for rewarding the participation of employees in the recruitment process. New approaches are explored to introduce scalability into recruitment from academic institutions.

❖ *Downward pressure needs to be placed on staff turnover* – this involves a wide range of interventions. The option scheme is going to help, but post-flotation the granting of options to new joiners has less impact than pre-flotation. Also, what happens when most of the employees are through their vesting period? Internal communication needs to continue to improve; I want to see this moving out of the calendarised cycles and into real time so that people really know what is going on rather than hearing about it later or reading about it in a monthly bulletin.

The change programme is all-encompassing. The HR director is not solely responsible for the programme, but many, many aspects of moving the business forward into the world of a public company with ever-improving performance involve the need for changes in the strategic management of human resources. The HR director literally needs to spend every day working on this project – not a formal change programme to solve a particular problem, but an informal strategic change programme to help the company move forward even more successfully. I would argue that this form of change programme is far more common than the single-issue formal BPR-based change programmes we all went through in the 1980s and early 1990s.

I do not need to look more closely at formal change programmes and HR involvement. Andrew has made this very clear in his earlier chapter – his description is binary; without HR the programme floundered, with HR it moved forward.

Custodian of culture

Describing this in terms of day-to-day activity is tricky. The role of custodian of culture has to flow through the daily activities. It means that when the sales director is busy convincing the board that it is correct to incentivise salespeople in a different way from other key people in the organisation, the HR director has already formulated a clear analysis of the impact on the culture, so that the board can make decisions with eyes wide open. It means supporting the director who doesn't want to offer a job to an extremely highly qualified person who is clearly not interested in stepping outside of his or her core discipline, or challenging the director if he or she is tempted to recruit the easy-to-manage people ahead of the proven non-conformist innovator. It means confronting people over screens between desks where open-plan is sacrosanct, over company cars where the history of the withdrawal of the car scheme is beginning to be lost from the collective memory of the board, and over many other issues that in isolation might appear petty.

In many of these areas we are providing an element of corporate memory to proceedings, running a fine line between the two George Santayana quotations:

> History is a pack of lies about events that never happened told by people who weren't there.

and

> Those who do not remember the past are condemned to repeat it.

Even the strongest and most popular organisational culture is a fragile thing. Small changes in the economy, the physical environment, the metrics, the performance of the business, the rules, the level of regulation, the communication channels (content or style) or even in the behaviour of high-profile individuals can have large, unpredictable and chaotic consequences. The HR director spends his or her day predicting these changes and responding accordingly.

Challenger of the operational status quo

The pursuits of the custodian of the culture often lead to challenging the operational status quo. This might be within the HR department itself or it can be challenging the assumptions of other directors or managers. It can mean challenging items that were once championed by the HR director himself or herself. For example, some time ago I pushed hard for the devolvement of bonus metrics into the operating units (for a very good reason at the time) and more recently have challenged this in favour of company-level metrics.

This is an aspect of the role of HR in today's organisation covered in Chapter 3; the entire HR profession needs to challenge such assumptions if they are to move their organisations forward. The only difference for the HR director is that it is the assumptions and myths of the CEO and the board that are being challenged.

Deliverer of resource

Finally, the HR director spends the day delivering resource. This might be budget or capital expenditure, or it might be people or time. The HR team needs to be able to access resource in order to operate. The HR director must ensure that the HR department achieves a level of reputation that makes effective resourcing a 'no-brainer'. Business cases need to be developed from time to time, but the status that really needs to be achieved is a level of trust that ensures that resource can be derived in real time, rather than through lengthy decision-making processes. This is one of the most important things the HR director can do for his or her team.

So how will things be different when you're on the board?

Professionally, one of the most memorable moments of the last few years was just before I was appointed to the board of Scientific Generics – the advisory and intellectual-property-generating company within the Generics Group. My training manager at the time asked me what would be different when I joined the board. Compared to my more recent experience of joining the executive board of the group, shortly after flotation, the answer could have been very little! However, there are some key areas of contrast between being an HR professional or even head of HR, and the experience for the HR function of working in an organisation where HR is recognised at the board.

I would summarise the answer to this question of what will be different in the following areas:

❖ representation
❖ understanding
❖ consistency
❖ business contribution
❖ collective responsibility
❖ paradox.

Representation

‘HR without board position is at an immediate disadvantage’

This refers both to the role of HR as employee champion and to the position on the board agenda. HR without board position is at an immediate disadvantage. How can we really be champions of employee motivation and morale if we do not sit at the board table?

Recently, I spoke at a conference and listened to a very experienced change manager describe a transforming board away-day at which there was no HR representation. There was no sinister reason for the lack of HR representation, only that this was a pending vacancy. But my despair at hearing this was almost audible among a polite HR audience. This was a watershed moment for the company concerned and HR lost the opportunity to represent the real people issues, or to represent the folklore of the away-day.

So being at the board means representing HR at the board. It means championing the employees at the board. But it also means representing the board to the rest of the company.

A seat at the board table gives HR issues a near-automatic right to inclusion on the agenda. At the board or not, recruitment and retention will always find their way on to the agenda, but all of us who have been non-director heads of HR have experienced the humiliation of presenting discussion papers on equal opportunity or the latest change in employment legislation to the board while they eat their sandwiches half-way through a gruelling board meeting!

Joining the board means being able to eat sandwiches with the best of them. It means no longer hearing someone say, 'We've decided that HR is going to. . .'. Being at the board means being part of the 'we'; this brings responsibilities as well as rights, of course.

Understanding

Joining the board feeds the understanding of business context that is essential for the effective delivery of HR strategy and tactics. Every good HR professional strives to understand the business context; I have described this as part of the role of HR in today's organisation and it is often cited as one of the core competencies of the HR professional. However, until you have one vote, just the same as every other individual at the board, on every issue, then the imperative and opportunity to understand is inherently limited. I'm pleased to say that the speaker to whom I referred earlier (the away-day that HR didn't attend) has achieved such a position in her organisation that she is now asked for opinion on the most obscure areas of organic chemistry – such is the esteem in which her board colleagues hold her input.

Consistency

By working with the board we are able to build consistency into the way we deal with human issues. Provided we are doing our job well, we can also almost guarantee a human element is built in to everything strategic from the beginning. At least if the HR element isn't built in from the start, we can never say we didn't have the opportunity to do so. Here we see responsibility sitting alongside our right to be at the board in the first place.

Not only do we find ways of achieving consistency across the business in terms of traditional HR matters, but we also have the opportunity to ensure consistency in other important areas, for example between internal brand and external brand. From time to time the board will embark on a strategic brand shift. Such an initiative will fail unless the internal employment experience of the people in the business is consistent with the brand the company aims to portray to the outside world. This may involve a formal change programme to ensure that the inside reflects the new outside, but as important is the intervention of the HR director to ensure that the external brand is reflective of the core capabilities of the organisation – or at the very least that the core capabilities stand a chance of changing to reflect the brand.

Business contribution

We ought to know quite a lot about the business of our organisation regardless of whether we have a formal position at the board. If we don't, then we have no place seeking a seat at the board. So we ought to be in the position of making a contribution to the business rather than simply looking at what the HR function has to gain.

Joining the board doesn't simply mean good things for HR; it can mean a whole new dimension to the strategic management of the business. No matter how well the board operates as directors rather than functional heroes, vested interests cannot help creeping into discussion at the board. This is true for every board I have sat on, whether voluntary organisation, educational establishment or business. HR has the opportunity to introduce an element of 'soft glue' (see Chapter 3 on the role of HR in today's organisation) to proceedings. The HR director has the opportunity to steer discussion away from the particular interests of particular functions and on to the common good. It takes an experienced practitioner to do this without appearing to simply be flying the HR flag.

Collective responsibility

In its most simple form, joining the board means never again being able to say that you are just the messenger. As a member of the board, the HR professional must be ready to stand firm with the collective decision. We can make all of the representations we wish within the context of the board meeting, but outside this arena we must stand up and be counted as a constituent of the message, rather than merely the interface.

All of the excellent HR professionals I have seen in action have done this anyway. Joining the board means there is no alternative. The aspiration of getting HR to the board does not mean we can revel in the self-satisfaction of having 'made it'; it means we have to accept our full share of collective responsibility, even when we might feel uncomfortable. Joining the board is the beginning of feeling uncomfortable, not the end.

Paradox

Here we have come full circle to the role of the board in today's organisation. The role of the board is to manage paradox. As I described earlier, the role of the HR professional fortunate enough to have achieved a board position for his or her function and himself or herself, is to take his or her place at the heart of paradox. This involves many complex balancing acts, but it is also the opportunity to make a significant and lasting difference to the fortunes of the business.

Developing an HR strategy

Since Clive's previous chapter concentrates on HR strategy, I will just add a few comments in the context of my analysis of the HR role at the board.

Any commentary on the role of HR at the board is incomplete if it does not consider the question of HR strategy. This is not a text-book on the subject, but we should examine the issue. In order to do so, we need a working definition of strategy, because it means so many things to so many people. One of the best definitions I have seen is from James Brian Quinn[5] in the Mintzberg and Quinn book *Readings in the Strategy Process*. Quinn describes strategy as:

> the pattern or plan that integrates an organisation's major goals, policies and action sequences into a cohesive whole. A well-formulated strategy helps to marshal and allocate an organisation's resources into a unique and viable posture based in its relative internal competen-

cies and shortcomings, anticipated changes in the environment and contingent moves by intelligent opponents.

Starting with this definition and finishing with a clear and agreed HR strategy is not, of course, a straightforward matter. I feel both comforted and disappointed by the recent work of Lynda Gratton *et al*,[6] who point out that:

> In fewer than half of the organisations we studied did the HR director play an active role in formulating business strategy, and there was only one instance of what might be termed a 'sophisticated' attempt to link business strategy to human resource strategy in the form of a written document.

So what does HR strategy look like and why is it not simply a big resourcing plan? And who determines the HR strategy?

The HR director is the focal point for HR strategy, but the strategy is part of the strategy for the company and is therefore the responsibility of the board. The HR strategy makes clear:

◆ *Priorities* – in line with the strategy for the business, what are the priorities for HR management? In my current organisation, these priorities are easily defined as the need to recruit and retain the right numbers of high-calibre people and the need to ensure a creative culture in a rapidly growing organisation. These are top of the list of priorities, and from these points the other elements of HR strategy flow.

◆ *Integration of goals and policies* – this is where the HR strategy differs from a big resourcing plan. It is the how, not the what. It is about integrating factors such as culture rather than the individual plans themselves.

‹ It is not a linear process starting with the business strategy and converting it mechanically into an HR strategy ›

The key issues for the HR director are the leadership and facilitation skills required of the HR professional, and an understanding of the strategy process. In particular we need to be aware that it is not a linear process starting with the business strategy and converting it mechanically into an HR strategy. It is a process that involves an understanding of the current and future strategy, a vision of the emerging themes of organisation and how things will need to be different, determining just how volatile the external environment might be and how the socio-economic expectations of prospective and current employees might change. It is picking a way through the commercial needs of the company, the need for corporate memory and learning, the state of the competition, the need for diversity and a home life for employees, and the need to interface with the market to achieve the level, quality and flexibility of workforce we need.

I advocate getting some of this down on paper (or whatever the intranet equivalent is), but I also advocate that getting it on paper is the starting point for revising and reviewing, and that the process leading to getting it down on paper is as important as the document itself. The HR director must drive, lead and facilitate this process, but participation in the process must be as wide as possible.

The board as a work group

This final, brief section points to the role of HR on the board in relation to the rest of the board. The board is a work group in the same way as many teams and groups are throughout the company. Ultimately the CEO is responsible for the effective working of that work group, but the HR director has a unique role to play in supporting this activity.

The board needs developing, resourcing and remunerating just as much as the rest of the business. The board members have 'welfare' needs and the need to discuss things with an objective sceptic or a sympathetic or empathetic ear just as much as the rest of the company. The HR director needs to be ready to shoulder much of this burden. However, this makes it even more important that the HR director understands the business and any inherent tensions.

The unique position of the HR director is that he or she is a part of the work group and therefore a constituent of decision-making and one of the individuals affected. Recognising the need for development interventions is important, though it requires a certain amount of exposure of personal development needs in order to get this on to the agenda. This is something that has a great deal of potential to be uncomfortable.

Remuneration decisions are perhaps the most stark area of paradox for the HR director. A properly formulated remuneration committee is of course an essential element of managing this issue, but the HR director still knows what and how the other directors are paid and all of the circumstances leading up to these decisions. The challenge for the HR director is to contribute objectively to the formulation of remuneration policy and decision-making, knowing that there is likely to be a very personal impact on himself or herself. This is simply an occupational hazard and it is faced by all HR professionals.

The answer rests in part in the procedures and processes in place to shield the HR director from decision-making about himself or herself, but it also rests in the confidence the HR director has in those ultimately making the decisions. The HR director has to lead by example in ensuring that directors have competitive remuneration linked directly to the performance of the company and in having the personal and professional integrity to ensure transparency, consistency and prudence in the remuneration policy. Ultimately the independent remuneration committee will impose these things, but better that the HR director insists on them in the first place.

The challenge for the HR director is to be simultaneously a part of a significant work group and to be supportive and critical of that group.

Summary

A place on the board is the ultimate accolade for the head of human resources and for the HR profession in general. It means we are recognised as playing an important role in the development of strategy and the strategic management of the business. This chapter identified and discussed key elements of what this accolade means in practice:

 The role of the board revolves around a number of paradoxes, and the HR director sits at the heart of all of these issues and needs to master the art of handling paradox.

 There is no clear description of what the HR director does all day, other than knowing that he or she will spend the large majority of time in meetings and other forms of dialogue. If the HR director is really going to make a difference, the difference needs to be made in meetings and dialogue. However, we can describe the networked mass of activities as: championing the needs of employees and organisation; managing change; acting as custodian of culture; challenging the operational status quo; and delivering resource.

 Achieving the position at the board table is not an end in itself. It is also not simply about changing title from manager to director. There are clear differences between the role of head of HR and the role of the HR professional on the board. These relate to the representation of HR matters across all business issues, building consistency in the application of HR strategy, understanding the business context, making a broad business contribution, taking collective responsibility for board decisions and moving to the heart of the paradoxes inherent in running a business.

 The HR director leads and facilitates the HR strategy process that makes sense of the future of the business in terms of both direct HR interventions and less tangible matters such as culture, volatility, change-orientation and attractiveness.

 The HR director sits in the unique position of having some responsibility for the resourcing, remuneration and development of a work group to which he or she belongs. This is the source of high potential personal impact. Developing the capability of the board and ensuring HR policies for the board that lead the way for the rest of the organisation can ultimately be seen as the essence of the HR director's contribution.

As I stressed early in the chapter, this is written from the standpoint of someone seeking to quickly develop as an HR director. It is not the finished work, more a setting out of the challenges ahead. Achievement of a seat on the board for HR directors is a great advance for the potential role of HR; all we need to do now is fulfil the potential.

References

1   GARRATT B. (1996) *The Fish Rots from the Head.* London, HarperCollins. p13.

2   *Ibid.*

3   LAWRENCE P. A. (1986) *Invitation to Management.* Oxford, Basil Blackwell. p27.

4   ULRICH D. (1999) *Human Resource Champions.* Boston, Mass., Harvard Business School Press. Chapter 5.

5   MINTZBERG H. *and* QUINN J. B. (1998) *Readings in the Strategy Process.* 3rd edition. London, Prentice Hall. p3.

6   GRATTON L., HOPE HAILEY V., STILES P. *and* TRUSS C. (1999) *Strategic Human Resource Management.* Oxford, Oxford University Press. p204.

Chapter 9

Making your organisation an employer of choice

Jon Sparkes

What we are trying to achieve

This book is about leading the HR department and about the implementation of leading HR strategies and practices. We have looked at the networked, chaotic environment in which HR is active today and examined the role of HR and some of the activities we have been involved in, both as individual HR professionals and as a profession. But what is it all about?

What are we trying to achieve, whose responsibility is it really, how are we going about it, and what does it mean for the HR function?

This chapter sets out an idea of what it is we are all trying to do. The phrase 'employer of choice' has been used for a decade or so as HR's entry into the corporate mission statements we use to try to give an indication of where the business is going. Whether our mission statements survive, we all still want to be employers of choice. One company I worked for set out its aim to be in the top five global deliverers of telecommunications systems. At the time we were something like number 14, and less than a year later we were part of number 3 – we had been acquired by one of the largest companies. Now, this didn't mean we'd necessarily changed anything for the better; the mission statement might be seen to be pointless, but we still wanted to be an employer of choice.

'The hypothesis is that all employing organisations must set out to be employer of choice'

In this chapter, the phrase 'employer of choice' is examined. The hypothesis is that all employing organisations, whether private, public or not-for-profit, large or small, growing or shrinking, must set out to be employer of choice. Clearly the definition is key; we can't all be *the* employer of choice, but we can all be *an* employer of choice.

While we talk of employer of choice, we don't always get our message across. I will look at the question of branding and how this affects and is affected by employer of choice strategies. In simple terms, if what we say we are isn't reflected by people's perception of reality, then we will have failed in our quest to be employers of choice. And if the branding of our organisation fails to reflect the experience and competency of our employees, then the external market will see through that soon enough.

So what has all this got to do with HR? In a word, nothing. Nothing, that is, if our definition of HR is the too expensive overhead function that constantly gets in the way of running the business. Nothing, if HR doesn't include the most important human resources managers, the people with responsibility for managing people – the line managers and, increasingly, the project managers.

We have advocated devolvement to the line for more than a decade, but only now are we beginning to realise what this might mean. HR makes itself redundant. But before the cheers ring around the organisations in which we work, I only mean the HR of the previous paragraph. In its place is something of far greater value to any organisation.

Clive looks at this change of emphasis for HR in greater detail in Chapter 1. The redundancy of HR is clearly described through the migration to the line and the introduction of technology-driven online services and outsourced services. While the new role for HR is leading the creation of a war room for masterminding the attraction, motivation and retention of staff in the twenty-first-century war for talent, the function has, in most organisations, made the shift from transactional to relational, and now we must lead the way into transformational.

What does employer of choice mean?
Recognising the need to be an employer of choice

Every employer wants to become an employer of choice. Before getting down to defining what this means, I will give three examples:

- a company (the Generics Group) at the heart of the hi-tech world, located in an area in which unemployment in the local economy is less than 1 per cent and the skill requirements are among some of the hardest to find in the world
- a large organisation going through downsizing and radical change in technology, processes and organisation
- a national not-for-profit organisation with premises across the UK able to pay salaries a little below national norms and significantly below the norms in a particular locality.

I will use these examples to demonstrate the variety of reasons that organisations have for wanting to become employers of choice, and to draw out common themes that lead to a working definition of employer of choice.

In the first example, the market in which the company operates is complex and competitive. It is complex in that the requisite skill base of the company already encompasses biotechnology, physics, optics, electronics, industrial design, mechanical engineering, materials science, communications technology, and battery and power source technology. It is competitive because it requires very high-calibre people in skills common to many of the world's growing businesses.

Employer of choice means a lot to this organisation, though it is not a phrase we particularly use. The average recruit has three or four offers to choose from, and only as few as that because the recruit has been very selective in the first place about the chosen company, sector or geography. Literally, the winner in this competition is the employer of choice for the individual concerned. How do recruits choose from three or four very attractive companies offering competitive salaries, a great working environment and massive learning opportunity? This is a question I ask people in final interviews. The answer is invariably:

- ◆ challenge
- ◆ variety
- ◆ people.

The final point gives us a clear Catch-22 situation, as getting the best people requires the organisation to have good people in the first place, or at least being able to demonstrate an intent to develop good people.

This gives a good steer in understanding how to be an employer of choice in this particular sector – sell lots of different and challenging work and employ the greatest set of people anyone could wish to work with. The choice for these people is stark: they do not have to struggle to find a job; they have to make a direct choice between several companies, all of whom are willing to pay them well.

The large, downsizing business was GPT Business Systems of the early to mid-1990s. GPT Business Systems was part of a company originally formed by the merging of Plessey and GEC's telecommunications interests. This part of GPT employed over 3,000 people, involved in developing, manufacturing and marketing business telecommunication systems. The downsizing was necessary due to the massive structural changes in the industry:

- ◆ The technology was changing so that business telecommunications systems were becoming more software than hardware – more programmed than manufactured.
- ◆ The market demand was changing from off-the-shelf to tailored.
- ◆ The environment of industrial relations was changing with the focus moving from adversarial industrial relations to employer–employee partnerships.

❖ Manufacturing techniques were changing to reflect the success of Japanese manufacturing firms.

❖ Requirements on employees were changing so that it was no longer acceptable to 'leave 90 per cent of your skills at home'.

Radical changes in the organisation were needed in terms of skill mix and cost base, and large-scale redundancies were necessary, alongside major changes in working practices and a redefinition of the role of the unions. At the height of the ensuing disputes there were several hundred industrial tribunal cases lodged against the company, which were eventually resolved after a High Court test case. So, how was this scenario relevant to the question of becoming an employer of choice?

This organisation needed flexible people, who worked collectively toward the eventual success of the business. It needed to break down demarcation and needed to come out of simultaneous recession and industry restructuring with a twenty-first century company ready to provide tailored systems to increasingly sophisticated customers against ever-increasing competition. It needed to retain good people.

As employer of choice, it provided new learning opportunities for people, engendered an atmosphere of personal responsibility, enabled flexibility in role definition, paid good market-based salaries and rewarded people with fulfilling careers, a sense of direction and the ability to make a real difference. There were many examples of enhanced careers despite the generally negative and demotivating atmosphere.

The point is that becoming an employer of choice remained a priority despite very difficult circumstances.

Finally, we consider the national not-for-profit organisation. The part of this organisation that I know about is located in one of the fastest-growing local economies in the UK. Unemployment in the sub-economy is negligible, house prices are growing faster than anywhere in the country and the organisation pays very low salaries. The need to be an employer of choice is paramount and money is not the answer.

For this organisation, employer of choice is about job satisfaction, prestige, geography and the opportunity to do something useful. The local management has recognised this and is struggling to achieve recognition of the issues among the national policy-makers. Movement in salaries would help and so would an integrated and emergent strategy for human resources. Again, the point is that becoming an employer of choice is essential and money is not necessarily the key.

A working definition

All employers need to become employers of choice. If they don't, they will not be able to employ the people they need to achieve the aims that all stakeholders have for the business. My examples demonstrate what a broad and bold statement this is.

A working definition for employer of choice might quite simply be:

> **An employer that the right people choose to work for … an employer able to satisfy the needs that its employees need to be satisfied by their employer.**

The challenge for the employer is understanding how to satisfy the needs in the context of the relevant internally and externally imposed environmental factors. All organisations work within constraints; they cannot all simply put in place perfect employment practices. They must however ensure that they think creatively and laterally in finding ways to overcome the constraints. In my experience, there are four key hurdles to be overcome in order to become an employer of choice:

 understanding the strategy and culture of the organisation

 understanding the specific people requirements of the organisation and the particular needs of those people

 understanding and responding to the underlying needs that people have in relation to their employment

 understanding something that can only really be described as the way the organisation works.

Strategy and culture

‘Maintenance or change of culture is likely to be the biggest challenge for the HR function’

Becoming an employer of choice begins with an understanding of where the organisation is going and why it exists – understanding the needs of all of the stakeholders. The purpose of attracting, motivating and retaining staff is the achievement of the business strategy. Culture underpins the ability of the organisation to deliver its strategy, and the maintenance or change of culture is likely to be the biggest challenge for the HR function.

In the Generics example, the ongoing ability of the organisation to enable, encourage and deliver innovation is at the heart of the business strategy. The innovation process is at the heart of the work the company does for clients and fundamental to the flow of licence revenue and the launching of a stream of spin-out companies. While innovation is key, it is certainly not something that can be engendered by the implementation of traditional *SMART* objectives. The answer is in the reward systems and flexibility in the metrics, but more importantly, it is in the assessment of innovations themselves. Innovations are peer-reviewed by a team of colleagues from across the business and, while the level of investment in the innovation and the magnitude of the reward is based on commercialisation, a significant level of recognition is also given for the quality of the technology in its own right.

Similarly, there are cultural aspects to becoming an employer of choice. The challenge for the company is providing an environment in which high-calibre people can constantly be challenged, can learn constantly, and have significant choice in the content and style of their work. It also means that people work in an organisation that treats them with respect, does not patronise them, communicates openly with them and propels them into situations where their input makes a real and sustainable difference to the clients they work for.

Of course, this is not only an inward-looking process. Strategy and culture are not absolutes but need to be understood in the context of the competition and the macroeconomic and microeconomic climate. In Chapter 1 Clive provides many insights into the need for the employer of choice to win in the war for talent. The HR professional needs to follow the competition and understand the economic trends that will have and are having an impact on the organisation. This is what I described in Chapter 3 as 'getting out of the office'.

Specific people requirements and needs

Armed with a clear, or at least emerging, understanding of the strategy for the organisation and the underpinning culture, the HR professional also needs to understand the specific skills and personal attributes required by the organisation and the particular needs of those people. This is the strategic equivalent of a job description and a person specification, but it is the high-level traits and needs.

The first part of this is often described as the core competencies of the organisation. However, this is not enough in itself, as employing people is a two-way transaction; we need to understand the core needs of the people and respond to those. For example, the career development needs of high-calibre, creative people may not be satisfied by a prescriptive one- or two-dimensional career path. Facilitating a flexible approach to developing the individual's career is something people look for. A business model that recognises that there are many ways in which the individual's talent can be applied to the development of the value of the business is a fundamental prerequisite to satisfying this need: all employers need people to manage people, manage projects, enhance the intellectual capital of the organisation, take a lead on new initiatives, deliver the day-to-day core business, provide professional support services to others in the business and find new ways of making financial gain for the business. Career development strategies need to recognise this multifaceted approach to business and should seek to guide without pigeon-holing.

Underlying needs of people in employment

There are specific needs the particular groups of people have, but I would also contend that there are underlying needs common to many people. They may only require the employer to satisfy a subset of those needs, but an employer of choice needs to recognise these needs and do something about them. The employer may adopt many different strategies to achieve this.

For example, the not-for-profit business I mention does not have to pay low salaries, but neither does it need to pay top-quartile salaries. Creative thinking in the use of volunteers and the effectiveness of the organisation may actually lead over time to employing slightly fewer people but paying those employees slightly higher salaries.

This is a single-issue example. A broader example is that of work–life balance. Achieving work–life balance is also important. The employment market for high-achieving technical people has reached such a level of selectivity that I have even known people to consider such factors as the optimal distance for cycling to work when deciding which employer to work for – and many more go as far as checking out what facilities are in place for showering and changing if they choose to cycle or to go running at lunch time. Work–life balance is about the individual balancing the needs that can be satisfied through employment with the needs that cannot. Many factors are considered – whether the employer respects the employees' need to spend time with their family, helps them to find information on childcare and educational facilities for their children, takes a positive view of sabbaticals for learning or travel, and recognises employees as a 'grown-ups' who can determine when to start and finish work.

The way the organisation works

In many ways this is a subset of the culture of the organisation. My experience is that the employer of choice wraps together aspects of culture and individual need into a project-oriented organisation. This gives people flexibility, an element of choice, responsibility and plays to their strengths. This orientation towards project and work content rather than hierarchy, function and status can be applied to any organisational situation. Those people with hierarchy, function and status may argue that their needs are already satisfied, but the employer of choice needs to spread satisfaction beyond those people.

For example, this project-oriented approach has recently been adopted by Opportunity Links Ltd, a small organisation for which I am a non-executive director. This organisation provides social information systems and services for local and national government initiatives and employs 30 people. The salaries in this organisation are respectable for the sector, but not directly competitive with the high-technology sector that dominates the local economy. My observation is, however, that it has some of the most talented and highly motivated people in any organisation I have worked with. The organisation and way of working they have introduced can best be described as follows:

- a structure that focuses on the market, with resource groups and resource managers building expertise in particular market areas – one local and one national in this case
- project orientation – everything that is done in the organisation is a project, managed by the most appropriate person and staffed by the most appropriate people without regard to their organisational 'home'
- the corporate knowledge of the organisation is built through semi-formal interest groups, with everyone participating and having a responsibility for building and spreading the knowledge of the organisation.

We did similar things at GPT in the early 1990s. As I touched on in Chapter 3 when describing the business partner in action, I worked with the head of the IT division to develop an employer of choice approach to managing the division. We had to achieve headcount reduction targets of almost 30 per cent and we had to achieve an organisation that faced outward to the rest of the company instead of the existing inward focus on the technology alone.

While achieving headcount reductions we needed to ensure that we retained the best people for the challenges ahead.

Simultaneously, we changed the management structure of the organisation and ensured that the management team was populated by people who could be relied on to develop the people in their team, provide them with a positive mix of new and challenging assignments, and promote a customer focus that had previously been missing. The technology-oriented structure was replaced by a clear customer- and employee-based organisation. We used a mixture of process mapping, counselling, structured interviewing and psychometric profiling to identify the best structure and the best people managers. I remember the point in the process at which we almost guaranteed retention of the most obvious up-and-coming star in the division. At a time of downsizing and tight cost control, this individual achieved a line management role and a significant pay increment. This was a great success in achieving employer of choice status in the eyes of this individual and those of many others in the division.

There were many other examples like this at the time. The transition of manufacturing processes from a traditional production line to a team-based cell system with individuals responsible for the entire production of the circuit board provided many opportunities for career enhancement. It also enabled the business to move from large batch manufacture to small batch tailored manufacture and to achieve the requisite cost and headcount reduction.

Headcount reduction may be a strange subject to end a section on defining and implementing employer of choice strategies. What is important in using this example is that the company in question did not simply offer larger voluntary redundancy packages that would have been popular among those who left and who typically would have been the most marketable people. A longer-term approach was taken that would retain corporate know-how and engender a new approach of flexibility. Mass headcount reduction is not a decision a company should take lightly, and it must be done in a consultative, transparent and sensitive way. The point is that it can be done in a way that contributes to a long-term employer of choice strategy.

‹We must know the strategy of the business and what this means in terms of the people profile›

The main contention of this section is that all employers should and can be aiming for employer of choice status, whether as a means for attracting new staff, retaining talent or building the capability of the business. My experience, and that of Clive and Andrew, is that this transcends industrial sector and economic cycles. We must know the strategy of the business and what this means in terms of the people profile, and we must become the employer that those people really want to work for.

Branding

Perception is, of course, everything. Many of the people at GPT in the early 1990s will find it difficult to recognise my description of attempts to become an employer of choice.

This is, however, more complex than simply ensuring that the internal communication mechanisms spread the message that the employer is doing these great things in its attempt to become employer of choice. People in the organisation, and potential employees, will be the ultimate judges of whether the organisation is indeed an employer of choice. One company, which may be seen as a direct employment market competitor to my current organisation, ran an advertising campaign on the local radio. The voice-over said that the best people to ask about the company were the employees, and the final comment the listener is left with is a voice saying, 'I'm really pleased that I chose to work for . . .'. The message behind the advertisement was fantastic: this is a place that people choose to work.

Advertising alone does not make a brand. The employment market requires branding just as much as the other market in which people and companies buy products and services. These two brands can be opposing, consistent or synergistic. Employees will compare the stated employment market brand with their real experience of working for the company. Beyond this they will also see differences between the sales proposition of the business and the internal workings of the organisation. I will use two examples from different industries and different economic climates – 2001 Generics in Cambridge and early 1990s GPT in the East Midlands.

Generics uses the strap line, 'Innovation is our Business'. This clearly describes both the added value the company brings to clients and the development of intellectual-property-based spin-out companies it creates. Is this consistent with the employment market brand, and is that brand consistent with the real life experience of employees? These are important questions addressed by the board of the company on an ongoing basis. The company does indeed have a reputation internally and externally for valuing innovation and producing radical solutions for clients. There are guidelines, almost design rules, that can be applied to the creation of innovative businesses, and in relation to people these include:

- Employing and valuing people who can be described as polymaths. This is a third category of people alongside the more familiar generalists and specialists. They have achieved excellence in more than one discipline, and consequently the likelihood of innovation at the interface between disciplines is higher when such people mix than for specialists with only one area of expertise or generalists who achieve a good all-round knowledge.
- Employing and valuing people who have a high degree of independence and a low requirement for rules, guidelines and structure. We all recognise these traits as not necessarily desirable, and certainly not easy to manage, but they are essential for an innovative business.

For the two brands (employment and sales) to coincide, and for synergy to be achieved, this organisation must ensure that people such as those I describe are recruited, retained, developed, motivated and recognised. At the same time, we need to ensure that these traits do not preclude commercial and client-facing behaviour. Quite a challenge, but in our efforts to become an employer of choice and achieve the commercial and cultural aims of the business this is essential.

At GPT in the early 1990s, a branding exercise led the organisation to define two interesting abbreviations:

◆ **G**etting **P**eople **T**ogether
◆ **G**rowth, **P**rofit and **T**echnology

The first was a superb piece of wordsmithing; the company developed, manufactured and marketed telecommunications systems,
pioneering the present and future means for getting people in
touch with each other. And great store was put by cross-discipli-
nary teamworking. Indeed, the very process for promoting this
brand internally involved groups of people from different departments and disciplines working together to build new approaches
for achieving the business needs.

Downsizing and attempts to redefine the relationship with unions
were huge distractions from what was a very positive process. But
even here there was consistency with the introduction of one of
the earliest and most innovative examples of broadbanding for
grading and salary purposes, establishing a new direct partnership
with employees and introducing new team-based manufacturing
processes.

It is not stretching a point to say that both of these organisations,
in very different circumstances, placed great importance on being
an employer of choice, being seen to be an employer of choice and
achieving a high level of complementarity between employment
brand and sales brand.

The challenge for the not-for-profit organisation mentioned
earlier is achieving the same mix of brands and real-life experience
of employees. The external brand is excellent; it is part of a
national organisation with a very prominent position in people's
minds, but one that perhaps needs some modernising. At the
same time the prestige of working for the organisation is good. I
understand that they are working on a programme to deal with
both their external reputation and their standing as an excellent
employer of highly committed people.

How many other employers could be said to be in the same position, and indeed, how long will it be before those organisations

that have got it right will need to look over their shoulders and see that it is time to do the same? This is a never-ending process: being an employer of choice does not happen by setting everything in place and then sitting back to enjoy the fruits of the organisation's labours. The organisation needs to attain a brand position that achieves the right reputation in the market in which the organisation sells and in the employment market. And possibly more important, we also need to ensure that the appropriate brand is recognised by employees as the organisation in which they work. We cannot afford to allow a dislocation between these elements; such dislocations are simply not sustainable.

What has all this got to do with HR?

I have described the imperative for organisations to become employers of choice. I have also indicated that this transcends the whole business, including the need to be integral with the ever-changing emergent strategy and the need for complementarity between the external and internal brands and the experience employees have of working for an organisation.

What does this mean for HR? My earlier chapters have considered the role of HR in today's organisations and examined the role of HR on the board, and Clive and Andrew have described both environmental factors affecting the HR function and some examples of the value brought to the business in leading change, developing partnership and establishing learning organisation processes and philosophies. But if getting to employer of choice status transcends the business, then what, if any, is the role of HR in this process?

After all, we have been chanting the 'devolve to the line' mantra for many years, so what is left for the HR function to contribute? A recent conversation with a colleague on the subject of staff turnover helps us to see through this issue. I was told in no uncertain terms that the only impact on staff turnover the business could apply was directly through the line managers. He said that nobody leaves a company because they don't like/agree with the HR director, and no one derives their motivation from the HR director or anything he or she does. This is brilliant news for all those HR people who have pushed all people management matters to the line managers, where they belong. This was one of those line managers saying that he was accepting full responsibility for all aspects of motivation, recognition, reward and headcount targetry.

It is true that people do not leave or remain with companies voluntarily because they disagree with HR policies, directors and managers. They work in an organisation because they believe that they will derive greater satisfaction (however defined in their own personal terms) or motivation in that organisation. This satisfaction is not derived from HR policy, director or manager. It is derived from their immediate work group and their personal experience of the workplace: how they are challenged or trained or paid, and how they think the business is managed. It is the behaviour of their immediate manager that has the greatest impact on their decision to remain with a particular company. For example:

- ❖ help they are given to develop their skills and careers
- ❖ enrichment or enlargement of their particular role
- ❖ interpretation of the organisation's policy on emergency child-care leave or flexible working
- ❖ feedback they receive on their strengths and weaknesses
- ❖ recognition and a sense of well-being in their immediate work environment
- ❖ perception of how the organisation is doing.

All of these things go on far away from the HR department in the operational areas of the organisation. Thankfully, the particular line manager I was speaking with also set out a role for HR in this process. Again, there were some examples:

- ❖ Who would push us to recruit increasingly outside the UK if the HR function did not advocate this approach, discover the appropriate channels for achieving this aim and ensure that they were tuned into the latest immigration and work permit situation?
- ❖ Who would codify important business people processes such as career development?

Who would do the thinking, homework and legwork behind the company's approach to share option allocation?

 Who would ensure that the business allocated sufficient resource to the development of leadership and management capabilities, especially when there was no overt demand for this from the line?

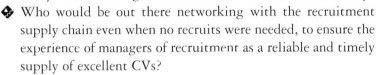 Who would be able to ensure consistency across the business in all aspects of reward and recognition – sometimes advocating prudence in the expectation and award of salary raises, and other times pushing for more frequent and more generous salary rises according to the state of the market and economy?

 Who would be out there networking with the recruitment supply chain even when no recruits were needed, to ensure the experience of managers of recruitment as a reliable and timely supply of excellent CVs?

 Who would have an approach ready to anticipate the growing demands from high-value employees for a greater sense of balance between their life outside work and their life at work?

And, in every case, who would challenge the line managers to ensure the success of each initiative? In many ways, this conversation sums up the contention of this book. Clive, Andrew and I come from very different industries and have very different experiences of HR. A common theme we have identified is the need for HR to be proactive. That is why the book is called *Leading HR* – it is about HR leading the agenda and leading their organisations in anticipating and managing change. Andrew identifies three very practical ways for HR to lead in organisations:

 The organisation that learns – Chapter 5 on the learning organisation describes the crucial role of HR in enabling the organisation to build both its body of know-how and a culture in which people see every day at work as part of their life-long learning experience. This satisfies so many particular and underlying needs of people and is a cornerstone of any strategy to become an employer of choice.

 Sustaining partnership – Andrew describes leading HR in one of the most difficult arenas, that of transforming the relationship between employer and organisations representing employees.

While Andrew describes the traditional arbitrative role of HR, he also describes how HR makes critical decisions and ensures that none of the parties involved loses the drive to succeed. This is a great example of HR leading an organisation towards being something resembling an employer of choice.

✦ *Change management* – once again, Andrew demonstrates how HR plays a leading role in change situations. Most change programmes fail because the people aspects are not part of the definition of the problem, the groundwork buy-in process, the technical consideration of the precise nature of the change, or the implementation planning and execution. Andrew demonstrates clearly how the opposite is also true – that most change programmes succeed when those aspects are in-built.

‹HR is more complex than the acquisition and utilisation of a resource›

From the list of activities in Chapters 3 and 8, and from Andrew's chapters (Chapters 4–6), we begin to see a concrete role for the HR function in making its organisation an employer of choice. The definition of the role of HR starts with the recognition that people are simply the most important asset in any organisation, and therefore a specialist business function is required to ensure that the organisation acquires, maintains, improves and protects that asset. This is the recognition that led us to the advent of HRM, but it does not lead us to a definition of the role of the HR function. HR is more complex than the acquisition and utilisation of a resource because the resource in question has personality, personal needs, a mind of its own, and most importantly of all it has legs!

The human asset requires care and attention. It requires recognition of its needs and an organisation that is able to satisfy those needs – hence my earlier working definition of the employer of choice. Satisfying those needs is far, far more than the old welfare specialism. A pure welfare approach in the modern world would not add value to the organisation because people would be led to believe that the organisation was there purely to serve them.

There would be no concept of rights and responsibilities; there would just be rights. As Clive sets out in Chapter 1, the HR profession has made great strides from welfare, through administration into generalism and specialism. It is now time to become business hybrids who can outsource and automate the support programmes and services and tackle the crucial issue of the talent war.

At each end of the spectrum from HRM to welfare, the line manager is the best person to deal with issues relating to the individual. The line manager is tasked with getting the best out of the people in the organisation (HRM), and the line manager is the best first point of call for any welfare matter. Other than guiding, developing and training the line manager, and ensuring that the metrics for HRM are clearly defined and that the organisation can access external resources to assist in matters of welfare, counselling and personal support, the value added from the HR function does not lie at either end of the continuum. There is a lot more to be done, and the function must not consider making itself redundant as a business function – though it should of course make a number of tasks redundant from its core activity through outsourcing and going online.

In managing an organisation, there are many levers those responsible for leading the company can attempt to use – increasing resource in the sales function or investing in new technology in the manufacturing area or undertaking a rebranding exercise. The HR function must be custodian of the lever-marked culture and it must put the achievement of the right culture for the organisation and its people at the heart of everything it does. This does, of course, involve many balancing acts, but there are several ways in which the HR function can fulfil its responsibilities in this area.

HR strategy

There must be an HR strategy. It doesn't always have to be written down and it can be a disadvantage to write something down that is out of date as soon as you stop writing. It has to be lived and breathed by the HR function, and it has to evolve as those factors upon which it is contingent themselves evolve. It must not simply be a reaction to some predefined, overarching business strategy, because that business strategy must be informed by a range of employment issues such as availability of resource and motivation of people, and will rely for its execution on the organisation becoming an employer of choice.

Outcomes, not efficiency

For businesses, winning in a market is no longer dependent on being able to beat the other guy on efficiency. Efficiency is simply a prerequisite for being in the market at all. Similarly for HR, being at the table is not a matter of being efficient. Efficiency is assumed.

So we need to ensure that HR measures itself on outcomes rather than process efficiency. Achieving 100 per cent completion of appraisals does not constitute success. Success is ensuring that the overall calibre and skill profile of the business has been applied to raise prices. It is not achieving a per head recruitment cost of 10 per cent less than last year; it is the achievement of the company's service level agreements due to the effective recruitment of excellent staff. Efficiency alone is not a valid metric; it is effectiveness and value added that bring organisational success and people motivation. We are better measuring employee perception and per head revenue than the number of hits on the recruitment website.

Socio-economic intelligence

The HR function must provide the organisation's eyes and ears on the employment market. The employer needs to be ready to deal with the socio-economic climate. This may be strategies to deal with the Government's approach to trade unions, the impact of a forthcoming recession, or a structural change in the industry requiring rapid changes in the skill or geographic mix.

I remember in 1988, as an undergraduate trainee, being asked to produce a thought piece for my boss at GPT on the employment consequences of the implementation of Japanese-style manufacturing practices, and wondering what on earth this had to do with HR (or personnel as we were called at the time). In 1990 I made a presentation to the trade unions to reassure them about the consequences of the forthcoming implementation of team-based 'U-Cell' manufacture. The link between the two events is easy to identify in retrospect.

Equipping the managers

While recognising the need for HR to look at the long term, we should not forget the short term. In Chapter 3 I described the role of HR in today's organisation. One of the most important contributions HR can make is in equipping line managers to deal with the complex morass of day-to-day people issues – equipping them in terms of their personal skills, information, support and advice, appropriate administrative systems that enable economies of scale, and mentoring. They do not want an HR function that interferes in their running of the business, but they do want infrastructure and assistance.

Conscience of the company

Effective management of culture requires a human dimension in every decision the organisation makes. The HR function must provide the conscience for business decisions by ensuring that the human dimension is understood and that the company really appreciates that satisfaction of the needs of the people is essential to achievement of business objectives. Promoting equality of opportunity and the work–life balance will only come from the HR function; subjects such as this will not make it on to the line manager's radar if they are not formulated and packaged by the HR function as issues that support the short- and long-term aims of the organisation. Delivery of the policy rests with line managers, but the HR function must position itself as custodian of the principles involved.

Professional integrity

Leading HR is not simply a matter of supporting the needs of the organisation. The HR professional must remain true to his or her profession and the people and business principles this represents. We have to ensure that our organisations are run properly and fairly, that natural justice applies to decisions about people, and that essential human rights such as privacy and the right to whistle-blow are retained. However, this application of our professional integrity must be intelligently applied and jargon-free. We have all had the conversation with line managers that starts with the sickening feeling that we are hearing something racist or sexist. We should stick to our guns and ensure that the manager knows that this is fundamentally wrong without burning bridges in the ongoing development of our relationship with the managers in the business.

Personal responsibility

Our impact on the development of the culture of the organisation will be stronger and more sustainable where our colleagues see that we are taking personal responsibility for the delivery of people and other business objectives. In my current role, headcount growth and turnover reduction are very visible business-related goals. These factors cannot be delivered by HR alone, but the HR function will have more success in achieving these goals if it stands up and is counted. Beyond this, the individual HR professional must stand shoulder to shoulder with the line managers and take personal responsibility for successes and failures in this area. We work through a network of influences and contacts, but if we don't take on personal responsibility then perhaps someone else should be given the responsibility. Culture is one of the hardest aspects of business to measure or manage, but I recommend that HR professionals volunteer, cajole and pester to be given personal responsibility for ensuring that their organisation has the appropriate culture. Delivery of such culture has a direct impact on the success of the business, and we should be at the forefront of that culture.

Integrate with the business

Finally, we must become experienced business people. We will deliver the HR agenda to the forefront of the business agenda only when we are personally recognised to have the business acumen to understand that agenda.

HR is dead, long live HR

It is not necessary for a business to have an HR function. The current HR function is based on an amalgam of historical decisions – for example, the introduction of trade unions, the recognition of psychology and other soft factors as influential on the performance of the work group, the advent of time and motion studies, the plethora of employment legislation and the recognition that people processes give competitive advantage.

Every individual aspect of the role of the HR function could be done by someone else, especially in the fast-moving, networked world of the twenty-first century. So is this the beginning of the end for the functional specialism? It certainly could be interpreted that way.

Needless to say, I don't think it is, and Clive and Andrew have indicated strongly that it isn't. We have much to do in developing and supporting managers, facilitating cross-functional initiatives, networking in the employment market, positioning the business internally and externally and contributing to the business strategy.

Functional specialism or not, however, HR professionals need to decide what it is they are going to do. Are we going to help the business to define and achieve its aims *and* represent the needs of real people, or are we going to allow our employers and the people they employ to miss out on fantastic opportunities for growth, prosperity and satisfaction? I think this is a very personal decision, but that the answer will be observed in our actions as a profession.

HR comes of age when and only when the business and its people and other stakeholders recognise that it has made things improve. This may be the achievement of headcount or a culture capable of delivering the business objectives, or it may simply be a sense that things are generally fair and consistent for people in the business, but it must be both the business and the people who recognise the contribution if the HR profession is to get and remain centre stage in the organisation.

❝Individual HR professionals must shoulder their share of the burden of non-HR matters❞

Individual HR professionals must facilitate, debate, challenge, support, deliver on promises, take risks, think out of the box, lead the way on people matters and shoulder their share of the burden of non-HR matters. Then they will make a difference, get recognised, enjoy themselves and further the reputation of the HR profession.

Individual HR directors must lead the HR function in the delivery of HR objectives but recognise that this is not enough. They must also elbow their way to the point where they participate fully in the leadership of the business.

This chapter, and the book, closes with a quote I read five years ago. It is as valid today as it was five years ago. Bonnie Hathcock was then the chief human resources officer at Siemens Rolm Communications Inc. in California's Silicon Valley. She was appointed to the role of CHRO with no experience in HR but 10 years' experience in sales and marketing for a Fortune 50 company and some multinational training and development assignments. She said:[1]

> This fluid architecture has abolished layers of management and those dreaded silos of compensation, benefits and the like. Out-of-box thinking and a cross-functional view of the business are the results. These are extraordinary times for the profession of human resources. The demands of the new century pose formidable challenges and exceptional opportunities. We must respond boldly and intelligently. Our corporate function has dwelt in the shadows long enough. This is the time for unabashed resolve. The next five years should be wildly exhilarating for those with the energy and drive to set the corporate world on fire.

There is massive potential for the HR function and individual HR professionals. The opportunity is there for us to make a big difference to our organisations and the people who work in them. I expect that the next five years will be as exhilarating as the last five years. Our challenge is clear; we must make our organisations employers of choice.

In achieving our challenge, we must forge ahead in two areas. In leading our HR teams to deliver ever-increasing value to our organisations, we must promulgate employer-of-choice strategies, management of culture and winning in talent wars as the key measures of our impact on the organisation. And in making HR a leading player in the creation of excellent organisations we must use leading-edge HR practices that enable HR to take a lead when and where it really matters.

Reference

1   HATHCOCK B. C. (1996) 'The new-breed approach to 21st century human resources'. *Human Resource Management*. Vol. 35, No. 2. Summer. pp243–50.

Index

With over 100,000 members, the **Chartered Institute of Personnel and Development** is the largest organisation in Europe dealing with the management and development of people. The CIPD operates its own publishing unit, producing books and research reports for human resource practitioners, students, and general managers charged with people management responsibilities.

Currently there are over 150 titles covering the full range of personnel and development issues. The books have been commissioned from leading experts in the field and are packed with the latest information and guidance to best practice.

For free copies of the CIPD Books Catalogue, please contact the publishing department:

Tel.: 020-8263 3387
Fax: 020-8263 3850
E-mail: publish@cipd.co.uk
Web: www.cipd.co.uk/bookstore

The E-Learning Revolution: From propositions to action
Martyn Sloman

ISBN: 0 85292 873 4
208 pages
234 x 156mm
2001

This seminal work by a top training manager and leading UK authority on e-learning is a call to arms to his profession. For too long, he argues, the agenda has been driven by IT; it is time for all those concerned with organisational learning and development to discard the traditional models, ignore the hype of the vendors and become active players in the connected economy. It cover:

- ✦ why barriers between knowledge management, performance management and training must fall to achieve competitive advantage through people
- ✦ how technology that offers learner-centred opportunities will redefine the way adults learn
- ✦ why expertise in 'soft' technology will give trainers new credibility
- ✦ what can be learnt from the different strategic responses to e-learning of blue-chip companies.

Chartered Institute of Personnel and Development

Customer Satisfaction Survey

The more feedback we get, the better our books can be! We will send you a
FREE CIPD MOUSE MAT (UK addresses only) as a thank you for completing this card.

Name and address: ....

....

CIPD membership number: ☐ ☐ ☐ ☐ ☐ ☐ ☐ ☐

1   Title of book..

2   Date of purchase: month .... **year** ....

3   How did you acquire this book?
    ☐ bookshop   ☐ Plymbridge   ☐ CIPD website   ☐ other (specify) ....

4   If ordered from Plymbridge, when did you receive your book?
    ☐ 1 week   ☐ 2 weeks   ☐ more than 2 weeks

5   Please grade the following according to their influence on your purchasing
    decision, with 1 as least influential: (please tick)

	1	2	3	4	5
Title					
Publisher					
Author					
Price					
Subject					
Cover					

6   On a scale of 1 to 5 (with 1 as poor and 5 as excellent) please give your impressions
    of the book in terms of: (please tick)

	1	2	3	4	5
Cover design					
Paper/print quality					
Good value for money					
General level of service					

7   Did you find the book: covers the subject in sufficient depth   ☐ Yes   ☐ No
                              useful for your work   ☐ Yes   ☐ No

8   Are you using this book to help:
    ☐ in your work   ☐ study   ☐ both   ☐ other (specify) ....

If you are using this book as part of a course, please give:

9   Name of academic institution..

10 Name of course ....

11 Is this book relevant to your syllabus?   ☐ Yes   ☐ No

Call 020 8263 3387 for our latest books catalogue. Don't forget, CIPD members get 10% off!

Any data or information provided to the CIPD for the purposes of membership and other Institute activities
will be processed by means of a computer database or otherwise. You may, from time to time, receive
business information relevant to your work from the Institute and its other activities. If you do not wish to
receive such information please write to the CIPD, giving your full name, address and postcode. The Institute
does not make its membership lists available to any outside organisation.

2299/09/01

BUSINESS REPLY SERVICE
Licence No WD 1019

Publishing Department

Chartered Institute of Personnel and Development

CIPD House

Camp Road

Wimbledon

London

SW19 4BR